Christianity No Longer Makes Sense

Evan Davids

Christianity No Longer Makes Sense

Copyright © 2017 Evan Davids

All rights reserved.

ISBN: 1547121939
ISBN-13: 978-1547121939

CONTENTS

1. INTRODUCTION

Life on earth is unbelievable. A pygmy seahorse, a Brontosaurus, a Neanderthal, a Venezuelan poodle moth — is this a joke? Seriously, where did this stuff come from? The staggering diversity of living beings is beyond my wildest imaginings, but how could even the simplest of life forms pop into existence? And how could consciousness possibly arise from mere matter? Think about that. How can a physical substance become aware of itself? And how then could a self-aware chunk of matter be emotionally moved by music, poetry, and sunsets? While the vastness of the universe is certainly mind-numbing and awe-inspiring, the ultimate enigma is that there is anything at all! Why is there something rather than nothing?

These questions bothered me from an early age. I didn't grow up in a religious home, but I assumed I would one day find answers in Christianity. Perhaps this assumption came from simply living in a predominantly Christian country, where churches are abundant and there's a Bible in every hotel room. Moreover, I, and just about everyone I knew, celebrated Christmas and Easter. Even if these were fairly secularized celebrations, I was still aware that they had something to do with Jesus, who had something to do with God. Given this cultural backdrop, I suppose the presumption that Christianity holds the answers to life's biggest questions shouldn't be surprising.

The idea of being a Christian was attractive to me. I was bothered that most people I knew, seemingly, were not bothered by the mystery of existence. I respected Christians for, seemingly, not taking existence for granted. One day I would be a Christian.

BUT (as you've been waiting for me to say), this day never came. When I eventually dove into Christian theology I was disappointed. Christianity didn't make sense — it might have made some sense a long time ago, but no longer.

How can I make such a sweeping claim? Which version of Christianity am I claiming doesn't make sense? I grant that determining the exact true form of a religion can be nearly impossible. Who gets to decide? A pope-like figure might be able to define the official beliefs of a religion, but there is no such figure heading the countless Christian churches and denominations. There is of course an authoritative book, the holy Bible, but Christians disagree about what it says.

That being said, a belief system cannot be endlessly flexible. If it could, naming it would be pointless. For example, an atheistic, white supremacist, anti-marijuana, reggae music hater cannot, in any meaningful way, be considered an adherent of Rastafarianism. Of course people are free to label themselves however they want, but without *some* parameters, labels become gibberish. So while the boundaries of a religion, such as Christianity, might be fuzzy, its core tenets are much less so.

Some of my commentary reflects the fact that my experiences center on Christianity in the United States, but the doctrines I'm critiquing have been consistently and officially believed by the major Christian traditions. I'm dealing with doctrines that have been upheld by church councils and official confessions of faith through the centuries. These are doctrines that if abandoned would flag a conspicuous shift from orthodoxy and call the viability of Christianity into question. I'm addressing the kind of Christianity that is believed (at least ostensibly) by masses of people.

Here is a portion of a rather traditional statement of Christian faith put out by the Evangelical Free Church of America:

> We believe that God created Adam and Eve in His image, but they sinned when tempted by Satan. In union with Adam, human beings are sinners by nature and by choice, alienated from God, and under His wrath. Only through God's saving work in Jesus Christ can we be rescued, reconciled and renewed. . . . We believe that God will raise the dead bodily and judge the world, assigning the unbeliever to condemnation and eternal conscious punishment and the believer to eternal blessedness and joy.[1]

This is standard theology, not just historically, but in today's largest churches (even if some of them are a bit shy about stating it plainly). I fully acknowledge that this statement of faith does not resemble the beliefs and teachings of *all* present-day churches. But this fact — that many churches do avoid, or even reject, core tenets of traditional, orthodox Christianity — actually supports my thesis. Let me explain.

Many Christian denominations liberalized in the 20th century. Emerging scholarship challenged long-held Christian beliefs and effectively changed the trajectory of these churches. If you happen to attend a service at one of these "mainline" churches today, you are not likely to hear about the need to be saved or Jesus' atoning death on the cross. You will likely hear a more earthly message focused on being a good person or taking care of the planet — content that could easily be delivered (possibly more effectively) in a non-Christian setting. To be clear, there's nothing wrong with drawing from the Christian tradition to create a positive message for the modern world. In fact, I'd be fine with all churches moving in this direction. The issue is, where does this leave Christianity? Is it just a vessel to communicate helpful moral guidance? Jesus can be a great

---

[1] "EFC Statement of Faith," https://go.efca.org/resources/document/efca-statement-faith, (April 19, 2017).

inspiration, but if the main goal is to encourage better behavior, why not also bring in wisdom from Plato, the Buddha, or even Tony Robbins?

Understandably, some Christians of a more liberal persuasion dismiss creationism, the atonement, or divine judgment as simplistic or archaic beliefs. Some claim that fundamentalists have hijacked their religion. But if they divest Christianity of these longstanding doctrines, they're left embracing something else. And what they're left with is not very clear. This problem becomes much more acute when the liberal church's very own *official* doctrinal statements mirror the beliefs proclaimed by fundamentalist churches. Even today's progressive United Methodist Church's foundational document, the Articles of Religion, is indistinguishable from the text found on a modern fundamentalist church website.[2] The Articles of Religion was written in the 18th century but nevertheless still enshrines the official positions of the United Methodist Church. The authority of scripture, the virgin birth, original sin, the atonement — it's all there, haunting the liberal pastor. If churches can't bring themselves to teach their official doctrines, they are tacitly admitting that their religion no longer makes sense.

So, my focus in this book is not directed at liberal forms of Christianity for two reasons. First, I find them too nebulous to pin down and critique. Second, their very existence supports my case. (See the Appendix for more on mainline Christianity.)

My target is conservative Christianity, formerly known as Christianity. While the liberalized mainline denominations are currently struggling to survive, the conservative, evangelical, Bible-believing churches are alive and well. I'm addressing their theology.

Whether Christianity, the religion about Jesus, hews closely to what he actually taught is a debated question. Perhaps a coherent and convincing reconstructed theology will emerge,

---

[2] "Articles of Religion for the Methodist Church," http://www.umc.org/what-we-believe/the-articles-of-religion-of-the-methodist-church, (May 5, 2017).

but formally disavowing beliefs that have defined Christianity for centuries is not easy. But before I get ahead of myself, speculating about the prospects for a new Christianity, I need to try to show that the old one no longer makes sense.

2. THE FALL

Unfalsifiable claims run wild and free in religion. If I tell you the unexpected nice weather on my wedding day only occurred because I prayed to Saint Medardus, you might disagree, but you can't prove my claim is false. Saint Medardus, who has long been deceased, operates "behind the curtain," in a realm to which you have no access. Admittedly, while I might feel strongly about the efficacy of my prayer, I can't prove my position either.

Beliefs about God commonly and comfortably live in this realm of the unfalsifiable. Decisively proving or disproving their accuracy is just not possible. Let's look at some more examples of unfalsifiable claims:

- God is three persons: the Father, the Son, and the Holy Spirit.
- Jesus is currently in heaven seated at the left hand of God (not the right, as most people think).
- God has a plan for you.
- God allowed 9/11 to happen as a punishment for America's tolerance of homosexuality.
- People who don't believe the above statements are being deceived by the devil.

- I was running late for book group. After I prayed to Jesus, I hit every green light! God never fails!
- I was running late for book group. I prayed for green lights, but God had other plans for me. He was totally trying to teach me patience. God always knows what's best!
- I never could have accomplished such a great feat on my own. All credit goes to God. He worked through me.

The inscrutable nature of such claims affords believers a lot of freedom and protection. Unfortunately for Christianity, not all its claims are immune from evidence. Christianity makes historical claims about humanity that were originally unfalsifiable, but now they are not.

THE FALL OF CHRISTIAN THEOLOGY

Senseless acts of violence, cruelty, and stupidity bring unthinkable misery to people all over the world every day. Parents are killed by murderers, drunk drivers, disease, freak accidents, and war, leaving small children orphaned. Kids are teased, abused, malnourished, kidnapped, raped and murdered. Anything you can think of, and worse, happens.

But suffering is not just a matter of humans poorly exercising their free will. A single mosquito bite can bring about terrible human suffering in the form of sickness, birth defects, and death. A quick internet search confirms the existence of a plethora of nasty creatures, such as the various parasitic wasps that paralyze caterpillars, ladybugs, and spiders. After rendering their victims defenseless, the wasps proceed to lay eggs in their stomachs. When the larvae hatch they feed off the helpless hosts' guts.

If anybody needs further reminding of suffering in the animal kingdom, YouTube is a great source. While writing this, I did a quick search and came across a disturbing video of a zebra struggling for its life as a crocodile ripped it to pieces. We might be quick to just accept that this is the cycle of life, but the zebra didn't seem to accept it. The crocodile needed to eat, but the zebra, not caring about the crocodile's needs, was desperately trying not to be eaten. And the crocodile clearly didn't care about the zebra's desire to avoid suffering and death. And let's just assume that instead of the zebra being in the wrong place at the wrong time, it was your best friend, or your best friend's baby. The crocodile would eat them both. This crocodile wouldn't care if it were baby Hitler or baby Mother Teresa. This gruesome contest of survival is built into the fabric of nature. Crocodiles, sharks, king cobras, hyenas, tigers, grizzly bears — they exist today because they are well-oiled killing machines. If they weren't so lethal they wouldn't exist.

Nature is indifferent. Natural disasters strike regardless of who might be affected. A forest fire might burn without endangering a single human, but roast a family of bunnies. A tornado might tear through an area with no one around to even take notice. A tsunami might pummel a populated area and kill over 200,000 people. Nature doesn't care about zebras, bunnies, or you.

Why would God create a world with so much pain and suffering? According to traditional Christianity, he didn't. We live in a fallen world. The paradise that God initially created is gone.

After creating the universe, including the first two humans, God affirmed that "it was very good" (Gen. 1:31). Everything started off "very good." The next two chapters of Genesis (the first book of the Bible) elaborate on the early days of existence. God made Adam, the first man, and placed him in the Garden of Eden. God instructed Adam not to eat from the tree of knowledge of good and evil, but besides that, this place was fantastic (fruit trees, no death or disease). God decided Adam should have a helper, so he made the animals. After appraising and naming all the animals, Adam wasn't quite sold on any of them. God then put Adam in a deep sleep, took one of his ribs, and formed Eve. Adam was satisfied. He named this new creature *woman*.

All was well in paradise until the couple disobeyed God, eating from the tree of knowledge of good and evil. This *original sin* changed everything! God cursed the whole of creation.[1] This event, known as *the Fall*, marks the point in history when sin and death entered the world and we, human beings, became distanced from God. Rick Warren, mega pastor and mega best-selling author of *The Purpose Driven Life*, explains:

> How did God let everything get messed up? It started with Adam. . . . Adam's sin became our sin — all of us. That sin has laid comprehensive and awful consequences upon humanity. For example, it has led to natural disasters and deformities. Nature doesn't act like it should. It often acts irrationally, complete with hurricanes, tornadoes, earthquakes, and planet-disrupting menaces.[2]

Because of Adam and Eve's original sin we now have natural disasters and deformities, but more consequentially, we are now stained with a sinful nature, which renders us all deserving of spending eternity in hell. The good news is God eventually sent a savior, Jesus, to be punished in our place. Jesus was crucified, and this blood sacrifice enabled God to forgive those who believe this story to be true.

> *Oh! precious is the flow*
> *That makes me white as snow;*
> *No other fount I know,*
> *Nothing but the blood of Jesus.*

The unchurched might mistake these lyrics for a death metal song, but in fact they come from a popular Sunday school song. The blood of Jesus washes away the curse of original sin and the subsequent personal sins of believers. The need for a savior is a direct consequence of Adam, Eve, and the Fall. Jesus'

---

[1] The biblical text cites some specific consequences for this first sin. God greatly multiplied the pains of childbirth. Snakes were cursed to slither on their bellies. Farming became very difficult work.

[2] Rick Warren, "How Did We Get So Messed Up, "http://pastorrick.com/devotional/english/how-did-we-get-so-messed-up, (April 25, 2017).

death and victory over death restored the broken relationship between God and humanity that resulted from the Fall. God doesn't have to damn everyone to hell anymore, even though they deserve it.

I want to be clear that these aren't just wild ideas cooked up by fundamentalists. From holy scripture to early church councils to official statements of faith (both Catholic and Protestant), the Fall and original sin

The First Few Chapters of the Bible.

Genesis 1: God creates the world in six days.

Genesis 2: Story of Adam and Eve living in the Garden of Eden.

Genesis 3: Adam and Eve eat the forbidden fruit (the Fall).

Genesis 4: Story of Cain and Abel.

Genesis 5: Genealogy from Adam to Noah's children.

Genesis 6-9: Noah and the Flood.

consistently undergird Christian theology. These doctrines are well attested across denominations and through the centuries. Let's quickly look at a few examples. In the Bible, the apostle Paul writes:

> Therefore, just as through one man sin entered into the world, and death through sin, and so death spread to all men, because all sinned . . . So then as through one transgression there resulted condemnation to all men, even so through one act of righteousness there resulted justification of life to all men. For as through the one man's disobedience the many were made sinners, even so through the obedience of the One the many will be made righteous. (Rom. 5.12, 18-19).

According to the Bible death entered the world because of Adam's sin. "For since by a man came death, by a man also came the resurrection of the dead. For as in Adam all die, so also in Christ all will be made alive" (1 Cor. 15.21-22). The apostle Paul also believed that the whole creation has been affected:

> For the creation was subjected to futility, not willingly, but

because of Him who subjected it, in hope that the creation itself also will be set free from its slavery to corruption into the freedom of the glory of the children of God. For we know that the whole creation groans and suffers the pains of childbirth (Rom. 8.20-22).

Church councils, which have been used through the centuries to formally define doctrine, have repeatedly affirmed and assumed the doctrine of original sin. For example, in the year 419, the Council of Carthage made clear that babies are born guilty because of Adam's sin: "Whosoever denies that infants newly from their mother's wombs should be baptized, or says that baptism is for remission of sins, but that they derive from Adam no original sin . . . let him be anathema."

The modern Catechism of the Catholic Church, released in 1992, continues to uphold the centrality of original sin:

> The doctrine of original sin is, so to speak, the "reverse side" of the Good News that Jesus is the Savior of all men, that all need salvation and that salvation is offered to all through Christ. The Church, which has the mind of Christ, knows very well that we cannot tamper with the revelation of original sin without undermining the mystery of Christ (389).

The historicity and centrality of the Fall is just as well attested in Protestant theology. Martin Luther and John Calvin, the two most important figures of the Reformation, believed in the literal truth and consequence of the Adam and Eve story. There are countless statements of faith, from past and present, that unmistakably affirm the importance and reality of Adam's sin, but I'll just offer up one more from Liberty University, the largest Christian university in the world:

> We affirm that Adam, the first man, willfully disobeyed God, bringing sin and death into the world. As a result, all persons are sinners from conception, which is evidenced in their willful acts of sin; and they are therefore subject to eternal punishment, under

the just condemnation of a holy God.[3]

Denominational variations of the doctrine of original sin exist, but for our purposes they are of little consequence. Christianity is predicated on the Fall and the consequent need for a savior. Adam and Eve were real people who were created in an idyllic state, but disobeyed God. We're now living in a fallen world and in need of saving. Some hold that we are born already guilty, as we were "in Adam" when he sinned. Eastern Christianity, which prefers the term *ancestral sin,* holds that we inherit the *inclination* to sin from Adam, but not his guilt. But East and West agree that Adam's sin brought physical and spiritual death into the world. And whether we are born guilty of Adam's sin or born predisposed to sin because of it, it doesn't much matter. Either way we're hopelessly in the same boat. Every single human being that God has ever created inevitably falls short of his standards. And the punishment for being as we inevitably are is damnation.

The point of all this, of course, is that Christian theology was built upon an event that never happened. There was no Fall. The historicity of Adam, Eve, and the Fall used to be unfalsifiable. But now, on this side of the scientific revolution, the biblical story has been independently falsified by multiple scientific disciplines. And without the Fall, Christianity doesn't make sense. Dr. R. Albert Mohler Jr., president of the Southern Baptist Theological Seminary agrees that this poses an existential threat to Christianity: "The denial of an historical Adam and Eve as the first parents of all humanity and the solitary first human pair severs the link between Adam and Christ which is so crucial to the Gospel."[4] Henry M. Morris, father of modern creation science, is also very clear about what's at stake: "If man did not really fall into sin from his state of created innocency, there is no

---

[5] "Doctrinal Statement," Liberty University, https://www.liberty.edu/aboutliberty/index.cfm?PID=6907, (April 25, 2017).

[4] R. Albert Mohler Jr., "Adam & Eve: Controversey Heats Up," August 22, 2011, http://bpnews.net/35973, (April 25, 2017).

reason for him to need a Savior. . . . If Genesis is not true . . . Jesus Christ himself becomes a false witness . . . Faith in the gospel of Christ for one's eternal salvation is an empty mockery."[5]

IT TOOK A WHILE BUT WE'RE HERE!

This (arguably) fatal flaw is a product of Christian theology being formulated at a time when people knew virtually nothing about the age of the earth and human origins. Since the scientific revolution, some 500 years ago, we have discovered facts about reality that the ancients couldn't possibly have known — one of the most disruptive being the notion of deep time. Multiple disciplines have independently uncovered the fact that the universe is very old. Humans, on the other hand, are a relatively recent arrival.

The first episode of the television series *Cosmos*, hosted by Neil Degrasse Tyson, helps us wrap our heads around the vast stretch of time that preceded *Homo sapiens*. By compressing the 13.8 billion year history of the universe into a single year (each month representing just over a billion years), Tyson powerfully demonstrates what a tiny fraction of the cosmic calendar humans occupy. So, if all of time is smooshed into one calendar year, midnight January 1st marks the Big Bang and midnight December 31st marks the present. We can then lay out a timeline of major events, putting the universe's history in perspective.

On March 15th the Milky Way galaxy forms. Our sun is not formed until August 31, followed by the earth and the moon. The earliest life forms show up on September 21st (10 billion years later). Sea creatures first crawl onto land on December 17th. Not until the final week of the year do we get forests, dinosaurs, birds, and insects. The first flower doesn't bloom until December 28th. At 6:24 am on December 30th (a day before the present) a giant asteroid hits the earth, spelling doom for the dinosaurs. Humans evolve in the last hour of the last day of the

---

[5] Henry Morris, *The Genesis Record* (Grand Rapids: Baker Books, 2006), 22.

year. We didn't start painting our first pictures until the last 60 seconds. Tyson wraps it up: "December 31st, 11:59 46 seconds — all of recorded history occupies only the last 14 seconds, and every person you've ever heard of lives somewhere in there. All those kings and battles, migrations and inventions, wars and loves, everything in the history books happened here, in the last seconds of the cosmic calendar."

The biblical authors had no idea about the universe's deep past. They had no clue about Neanderthals or any other early hominid. They had no clue that earth was home to countless species experiencing death and extinction for more than 3 billion years prior to the emergence of *Homo sapiens*. It's not because they were dumb. They just lived a long time ago, before we had access to this information. The problem for Christians of course is that the Bible is believed to be much more than just the musings of an ancient culture: it's the Word of God.

YOUNG EARTH CREATIONISM

God created the heavens, the earth, plants, animals, and the first humans in 6 days. God declared everything "very good." Adam and Eve had it made in the shade until they chose to ruin everything for everyone. Rick Warren explains how it used to be: "Before sin, there was no death in the world. There was no sadness in the world. There was no sorrow. There was no difficulty in the world. People would not die. Adam and Eve could have lived forever as long as it was a perfect environment. It was only when everything got broken that sin brought death into the world." There's really no place for billions of years of survival-of-the-fittest in this picture. This traditional view has come to be known today as young earth creationism. And there's very good reason to believe in a young earth, if you believe the Bible is the word of God.

It's doubtful the Bible would say, "In the beginning God created the heavens and the earth," if it actually meant, "In the beginning God created the heavens and 10 billion years later created the earth." It would be extraordinary if the Bible did say that! Regarding the institution of marriage, the Bible says, "From the beginning of creation, God made them male and female" (Mark 10.6). Did the author actually mean, "In the latter parts of creation, God made them male and female"? Either *beginning* actually means *beginning*, or this is sloppy writing.

So how old is the earth according to the Bible? A straightforward reading of the text dates it at around 6,000 years. Since science has uncovered an old earth, some Christians have tried their hardest to read billions of years into the text (more on that later). But without science dirtying the calculation, God created the universe, earth, and life a mere 6,000 years ago. This number is derived largely from the genealogies provided in the Bible, which begin with the first man, Adam.

The genealogies not only give us each patriarch's age at death, but also the age at which he fathered the next person in the genealogy. For example, Genesis 5 informs us not only that Adam lived to be 930 years old, but that he fathered his son Seth when he was 130 years old. Seth then lived to be 912 years old and fathered Enosh at the age of 105. Enosh then fathered Kenan at the tender age of 90. Generations later we get to Noah and the story of the Flood. The genealogy picks back up in Genesis 11 in the same manner. Eventually we get to Abraham (as in the patriarch of the Abrahamic religions: Judaism, Christianity, and Islam). With a little math, we learn that Adam was created approximately 2,000 years before Abraham.

The New Testament also contains genealogies. Matthew charts Jesus' lineage back to Abraham (Matt. 1.1-16) and Luke connects Jesus' lineage all the way back to Adam (Luke 3.23-38). These genealogies don't provide us with ages like the ones in Genesis do.[6] But, by mapping out events such as the Exodus and the reigns of certain kings, most Christians estimate Abraham and Jesus are about 2,000 years apart. Therefore, the time between Creation and Abraham is roughly 2,000 years, Abraham to Jesus is roughly 2,000 years, and Jesus to the present is

---

[6] Matthew's and Luke's genealogies don't jibe with each other, but for theological reasons, they both make sure Jesus descended from King David.

roughly 2,000 years. Estimates for the date of Creation have consistently hovered around 4000 BC.[7] In fact, for a long time the King James Bible was printed with annotations citing a creation date of 4004 BC.

The main problem with young earth creationism is that it has been utterly destroyed by science. A long time ago it wasn't absurd, but now it is. The fact that the earth is vastly older than a few thousand years is so thoroughly established that I don't feel much need to defend it here, but I'll mention a few things.

We can see stars that are millions of light years away, which means that light has been traveling for millions of years to reach us. When astronomers witness the explosion of a supernova from one of these distant stars, they are witnessing an event that actually happened millions of years ago.

Deep ice cores, which are extracted by drilling down into sheets of ice, reveal annual layers going back hundreds of thousands of years. By simply counting the annual layers (similar to counting tree rings), one can safely conclude that the earth is much older than 6,000 years. The age of these layers is not only corroborated by radiometric dating, but also by known volcanic activity. For example, we know Mount Vesuvius erupted in the year 79. Scientists would then expect to find volcanic ash present in the layer that was laid down in the year 79 — and that's exactly what they do find. Geologic examples of an old earth are plentiful.

The fossil record bears out the story of life nicely. Simpler and more primitive organisms are consistently located down in the older, lower rock layers. Hominids, for example, are not. They're found up in the newer layers. Transitional fossils are found right where they should be. The more recent fossils most

---

[7] Calculations using the Septuagint, which is the Greek translation of the Hebrew scriptures (Old Testament) that was widely used during the New Testament period, push the date of creation back some 1,500 years to around 5500 BC. The ages in the Septuagint's genealogies differ from those in the Hebrew Masoretic text. Protestants, which pretty much all young earth creationists are, hold the Masoretic text to be more authoritative.

closely resemble species alive today. Radiometric dating and modern genetic testing both corroborate this gradual evolution we find in the fossil record. This consistent ordering in the strata makes no sense if all living things were created at the same time.

Within their diminutive timeline, young earth creationists must also account for the vast array of established and disparate cultures spread across the globe. And this problem is even worse than one might think. In the Bible Adam and Eve start the human race, but later there's a flood that wipes the earth clean. As the only survivors, Noah and his family have to restart the human population: "The sons of Noah who went out of the ark were Shem, Ham, and Japheth. . . . These three were the sons of Noah; and from these the whole earth was peopled" (Gen. 9.18-19). Therefore, according to the Bible, all humanity fans out from an even more recent date: about 2400 BC.[8]

Can you imagine a history class that taught that around 2400 BC there was a worldwide flood that wiped out the entire world? No. What was actually happening around the globe at this time? The Egyptians had a robust culture with some large pyramids. Stonehenge was taking shape in Britain. China had long been a civilizational hot spot. The Sumerians were thriving. Myriad tribes and cultures were spread across the Americas, Africa, and Australia. Things were happening in every region of the world with no sign of interruption by a global flood.

To be a young earth creationist one must believe that dinosaurs and humans lived together a few thousand years ago. One must believe that there was no death prior to human sin. One must believe that the disciplines of astronomy, geology, paleontology, biology, archeology, and history, which all independently collide with the young earth model, are massively wrong (we're talking deep, widespread incompetence, or perhaps a worldwide cross-disciplinary conspiracy to undermine the Bible).

If you happen to believe the world is 6,000 years old, your

---

[8] Birds and land animals also have to start multiplying all over again.

faith rests upon a worldview that has been demolished by science. No university on the planet (except a handful of fundamentalist schools) is debating the merits of a young-earth position. And it's not just universities; the fact that dinosaurs lived millions of years ago is uncontroversially taught from kindergarten on up.

This is not to say that young earth creationists are simpletons. Not at all. There are brilliant creationists who fight valiantly to explain away the mountains of evidence for an old earth. It's not an easy job, but they simply can't afford to be wrong on this one. There's too much on the line. People will go to great lengths to preserve their faith. It's their identity. It's what they've wagered their entire lives upon, and is therefore often non-negotiable. From the young earth perspective, scientific evidence must take a back seat to God's Word.[9]

GAME OVER?

So if Christianity's Achilles has been snipped, why is it still standing? I would venture to guess that part of the reason is that many believers just don't spend much time connecting the theological dots. If Christians are scarcely aware of the problem, then they can carry on unperturbed. In many cases, the people in the pews can't be blamed, as pastors regularly tip toe around the land mines.

What does Jesus' saving act on the cross mean if there was no Fall? Does the Christian story still make sense in light of evolution? In light of a 4.5 billion year old earth?

While rank-and-file Christians might not often dwell on these questions, some faithful scholars do. The problem of Christianity surviving without the Fall is acutely felt by many leading thinkers in the evangelical world. One such Christian is

---

[9] Christians have been able to shed belief in other scientific inaccuracies, such as the biblical view that the sun travels around a stationary earth, by reinterpreting passages as poetic. But Christians don't have that same luxury with Adam, Eve, and the Fall, because they are deeply embedded in the Christian narrative.

apologist (an apologist is a defender of the faith) Fazale Rana, who states, "But if the parts of Scripture that you are claiming to be false, in effect, are responsible for creating the fundamental doctrines of the Christian faith, then you've got a problem."[10]

One solution, as we've seen, is to reject the science, no matter what. As science (and biblical scholarship) continued encroaching on traditional beliefs, fundamentalism arose. Christians drew a line in the sand, declaring "enough is enough!" Henry Morris exemplified this sentiment: "By all means, therefore, we must oppose any effort from any source to mythologize or allegorize the Genesis record."[11] Creationists such as Morris have fought tirelessly to keep the young earth position viable, but modern science offers it little chance of recovering any ground. Aware of this reality, evangelical Christians are increasingly deserting the young earth position, but can they embrace science while credibly keeping the Christian story intact? The next two chapters explore this question.

---

[10] Quoted by Barbara Bradley Hagerty, "Evangelicals Question the Existence of Adam and Eve," http://www.npr.org/2011/08/09/138957812/evangelicals-question-the-existence-of-adam-and-eve (April 25, 2017).

[11] Morris, 22.

3. ADJUSTING FOR AN OLD EARTH

Prior to the emergence of human beings, the same uncaring contest for survival that we see in nature today had been raging for billions of years. This picture looks nothing like the one described in the Bible, in which there is a first human couple, created in an unspoiled state a few thousand years ago, who caused the world to instantly descend into the imperfect world that we live in today. Christians have been faced with three options: hunker down and ignore/reject the science, admit that the Bible is wrong, or seek out new biblical interpretations that can coexist with science. As the old proverb goes, "Necessity is the mother of invention." Enter *old* earth creationism. Old earth creationists attempt to maintain the historicity of Genesis while accepting scientific dating.

GAP THEORY

In response to breakthroughs in geology in the 19th century, a version of old earth creationism known as the *gap theory* gained popularity. The gap theory asserts that there were actually two creation periods with millions of years in between. God created the heavens and the earth, some sort of cataclysmic event wiped the world clean, and *then* the six day creation described in the Bible began. In other words, we're living in a second creation of sorts. The first creation is responsible for all those weird fossils that don't resemble today's animals (dinosaurs, giant sloths, etc.) and also accounts for the geologic evidence of an old earth. So where does this large gap of time fit into scripture? Let's look.

Gen. 1.1	In the beginning God created the heavens and the earth.
Gen. 1.2	The earth was (became)[1] formless and void, and darkness was over the surface of the deep, and the Spirit of God was moving over the surface of the waters.
Gen. 1.3	Then God said, "Let there be light," and there was light

The alleged gap lies between the very first two verses of the Bible, Genesis 1.1 and 1.2 . This new interpretation held that a cataclysmic event made God's creation "formless and void" (usually speculated to be "Lucifer's flood," an event resulting from Satan's supposed rebellion). The next verse, Genesis 1.3, then begins day one of the new creation. By having an initial creation that got wiped clean, believers were able to accept an old age for the earth while preserving the traditional six day creation that brought about our current world.

This theory has few subscribers today. Critics point to the obvious fact that the Bible never makes mention of a "restart." Billions of years of animal death and extinction, a rebellion in heaven, and crushing judgment strewn across the earth would be a lot to leave out between verses. And the text doesn't read like a do-over. God isn't said to be recreating or remaking the heavens. And animals and plants are depicted as new things. Furthermore, the next book of the Bible (Exodus) includes "the heavens and the earth" as part of the six days: "For in six days

---

[1] Gap theory proponents translate Genesis 1:2 as "The earth *became* formless and void, and darkness was over the surface of the deep, and the Spirit of God was moving over the surface of the waters" (i.e. *was* is changed to *became*).

the LORD made the heavens and the earth, the sea and all that is in them, and rested" (Exod. 20:11).

The other major problem with the gap theory is that it still doesn't jibe with geology. The entire reason for proposing it in the first place was to accommodate geological findings. But geology reveals a long gradual process leading to the present. There was no absolute demolition that left the earth formless and void and there was no recent restoration of the cosmos or the earth.

DAY-AGE THEORY

Today's most popular version of old earth creationism is known as the *day-age theory*, which has been most successfully propounded by an organization called Reasons To Believe (RTB). RTB was founded by Hugh Ross, who holds a PhD in Astronomy. The organization does not embrace evolution, but generally accepts scientific ages for the universe, earth, and life. Ross and his colleagues have worked out an impressively creative framework that attempts to harmonize the Bible with an old earth. They strive to preserve the historicity of the book of Genesis, and Adam and Eve specifically, while sparing Christianity the embarrassment of a 6,000 years old earth. In the words of RTB Vice President and biochemist Fazale Rana, "From my viewpoint, a historical Adam and Eve is absolutely central to the truth claims of the Christian faith."[2]

As the name suggests, the day-age theory interprets the "days" of creation described in Genesis 1, not as literal days, but as long "ages." The Hebrew word for *day* is *yom*, which, like in English, has various definitions but most commonly refers to a 24-hour period. *Day* can sometimes mean *a period of time*: "Back in my day, kids played outside." *Yom* can be used similarly in Hebrew. Context determines the meaning.

---

[2] Quoted by Barbara Bradley Hagerty, "Evangelicals Question the Existence of Adam and Eve," http://www.npr.org/2011/08/09/138957812/evangelicals-question-the-existence-of-adam-and-eve (April 25, 2017).

Did the ancient author of Genesis 1 actually intend for the six-day creation to be interpreted as six periods of millions or billions of years each? Very doubtful. Oxford Old Testament scholar James Barr found this interpretation unconvincing and motivated by necessity: "They shifted their interpretation of the Bible passage from literal to non-literal in order to save that which for them was always paramount, namely inerrancy of the Bible"[3] (inerrancy is the belief that the biblical writings contain no errors). Young earthers, of course, find this move dubious too. They point out that whenever *yom* is used with a number (e.g. *second* day), or in the context of *evening* or *morning*, as it is in Genesis, it always means an ordinary 24-hour day.[4] As I noted last chapter, inserting billions of years into the text is a hard sell. Verses such as, "From the beginning of creation, God made them male and female," or "For in six days the LORD made the heavens and the earth, the sea and all that is in them" make it hard to believe the authors had a multi-billion year process in mind.

I have to side with the young earth creationists on this one, but let's assume *yom*, in the Genesis 1 context, does mean *vast period of time*. RTB's day-age theory then must correlate the biblical days of creation with earth's actual history. Meeting this challenge requires a little faith and some massaging of the text. For example, on day three, God separated the waters from dry land and then called forth vegetation and fruit trees. On day four, "God made the two great lights, the greater light to govern the day, and the lesser light to govern the night; He made the stars also. God placed them in the expanse of the heavens to give light on the earth" (Gen. 1.16-17). The Bible wrongly claims the sun (the greater light) was created after the earth. To rectify this, RTB claims that the sun was indeed created before the earth, but was hidden from earth due to the thickness of the planet's early

---

[3] James Barr, *Fundamentalism* (Philadelphia: Westminster Press, 1978), 42.

[4] Ken Ham, "The Necessity for Believing in Six Literal Days," 1995, https://answersingenesis.org/why-does-creation-matter/the-necessity-for-believing-in-six-literal-days, (May 12, 2017).

atmosphere, which then dissipated on "day" four.[5] They argue that from the vantage point of earth's surface, the sun was new.

RTB also knows fruit trees are a relatively recent arrival on earth, so they must explain the Bible's claim that fruit trees (day three) emerged prior to animals (days five and six). RTB's model conveniently allows for "days" to overlap. This allowance definitely widens the goal posts (day three, for example, leaks all the way into day six). Similarly, there's the problem of insects being created after plants in the Bible. RTB explains, "Since insects play a critical role in the pollination of many plants, we are left with two possibilities: either God

PROGRESSIVE CREATIONISM

Most day-age adherents also identify as progressive creationists, which means they believe God has gradually introduced new plants and animals onto the planet. The gradual process of new species emerging, as revealed in the fossil record, is usually associated with evolution, but not in this case. Over the last few billion years, the theory goes, God has been periodically releasing new species into the wild. Progressive creationists don't tend to talk about what these intermittent creation events might look like, but I can only imagine they're quite a sight! Imagine a fully formed species materializing out of thin air. Poof! Birds exist. Millions of years later . . . Poof! Monkeys are swinging from the trees. I imagine such an event could be a bit unsettling for the existing wildlife in a given ecosystem. Poof! T. rexes are on the loose. Alternatively, God could have used *some* evolution, but at various points imposed radical, species-wide genetic alterations that would result in the birth of a new species (e.g. reptiles hatching birds).

created plants and insects together, or God pollinated the plants until insects were created."[6] I guess God can always fill in the gaps until the requisite pieces are in place. The Bible also defies science by declaring that birds were created prior to land animals. This claim requires further interpretive gymnastics.

---

[5] Greg Moore, "Does Old-Earth Creationism Contradict Genesis 1," March 1, 2007, http://www.reasons.org/articles/does-old-earth-creationism-contradict-genesis-1-2, (May 12, 2017).

[6] Ibid.

The problem is that the Bible is supposed to be the word of God. If the Creator of the universe authors a book, we should be blown away by its accuracy, not squinting our eyes, trying to make it barely make sense. Why would God want to mislead and confuse people?

WHY WOULD GOD CREATE SO MUCH DEATH, SUFFERING, AND WASTE?

One consequence of accepting the geologic record, is that millions and millions of species were created and then snuffed out well before the arrival of Adam and Eve. The traditional view of death and "natural evil" (predation, hurricanes, drought, etc.) entering the world as a consequence of the Fall cannot be maintained. From the young earth perspective, this is an inexcusable flaw in the old earth worldview. They argue that this is not only unbiblical, but it impugns God's character. Why would God create a world in which death and suffering are built into the very fabric of nature? And why would God then call it "very good"? Why create countless species over billions of years that will just go extinct long before the show even starts? Furthermore, if the world looks pretty much the same now as it did before the Fall, doesn't this water down the Christian message? Famed young earth creationist Ken Ham explains:

> The Bible is adamant though, that death, disease, and suffering came into the world as a result of sin. God instituted death and bloodshed because of sin so man could be redeemed. As soon as Christians allow for death, suffering, and disease before sin, then the whole foundations of the message of the Cross and the Atonement have been destroyed. The doctrine of original sin, then, is totally undermined. If there were death, disease, and suffering before Adam rebelled—then what did sin do to the world? What does Paul mean in Romans 8 when he says the whole of creation groans in pain because of the Curse? How can all things be restored in the future to no more death and suffering, unless the beginning was also free of death and suffering?[7]

---

[7] Hamm.

RTB responds to these criticisms by drawing a sharp line between the death and suffering of humans (*Homo sapiens*) and animals.[8] Human death, they argue, is indeed a result of the Fall, but zebras, bunnies, Neanderthals and all the other creatures were never intended to be sheltered from suffering and death. They're in an entirely different category. After all, Jesus didn't die to save the souls of animals. Humans are the relevant species, and the only one capable of sinning.

But an old earth does change the Christian narrative. Predation, tsunamis, drought, and disease become part of God's original design. Narrowing the impact of the Fall and shifting responsibility for these phenomenons from humans (Adam and Eve) over to God makes some Christians very uncomfortable, and understandably so.

Creationists, young and old, do agree that humans, who are created in the image of God, are the ultimate purpose of God's creation. The Bible never discusses a vast history of animal life prior to Adam and Eve (again, this would be remarkable if it did!). The Bible is clearly about the human race and God. Given this fact, having 99 percent of species that ever lived go extinct before the story even begins seems a bit odd (and wasteful). And why all the gratuitous suffering? Under the progressive creationist model, God gradually releases his newest designs into the world (as if it were a giant coliseum) to battle it out for survival. For millions of years the unfit and the unlucky have been eaten by predators, starved to death, and drowned by tsunamis. Was this divine entertainment? The prelims?

RTB rebukes such criticisms for having the audacity to question God's ways.[9] Who are we to critique God's methods? If God wants crocodiles to snack on live zebras, that's his call. This is how the all-knowing creator chose to create — and you with your fallen little brain are judging him? But as a second line of

---

[8] Greg Moore, "Old-Earth Creationism: A Heretical Belief?" August 23, 2007, http://www.reasons.org/articles/old-earth-creationism-a-heretical-belief, (May 12, 2017).

[9] Ibid.

defense, they do offer some possible reasons for why God might have created all those species that were extinguished prior to Adam and Eve's arrival.

In slight contrast to my *Hunger Games* hypothesis above, RTB suggests God might have created all these millions of species through the eons for artistic purposes. As a Creator, God naturally finds enjoyment in the creative process. From the platypus to the Denisovan, these life forms are forms of expression for the Creator.[10] Alternatively, they suggest the vast history of life on earth was needed to prep the way for humans: "A healthy ecological system depends on a continuing cycle of life and death. Also, many things that are important to human life — coal, oil, limestone, topsoil to name but a few — all come from the death and decay of animals."[11]

The implication here seems to be that God *needed* billions of years, death, and decay, because that's how nature works in our world. But isn't God the one who dictates how nature works? Is there some sort of rule book for creator gods that dictates certain requirements? "Rule 1: A healthy ecological system must include death and suffering (mosquitos, volcanos, and the flu are not required, but recommended). Rule 2: A proper creation must include fossil fuels (remember, there are no shortcuts here; fossil fuels take millions of years to make, so plan accordingly)." Maybe being all-powerful isn't all it's cracked up to be. Further undercutting this position is RTB's own belief that there will come a time when "The wolf and the lamb will graze together, and the lion will eat straw like the ox." So apparently they do believe God can create a non-carnivorous ecological system.[12]

Not all old earth creationists have made peace with the idea that natural evil comes directly from God. William Dembski, one of the leaders of the Intelligent Design movement, states, "A world in which natural evils such as death, predation,

---

[10] Fazale Rana on *Unbelievable?*, Podcast audio, September 25, 2015. Also *I Didn't Know That*, Podcast audio, June 11, 2013.

[11] Moore.

[12] Hugh Ross, *The Genesis Question* (Colorado Springs, Navpress, 1998), 98.

parasitism, disease, drought, floods, famines, earthquakes, and hurricanes precede humans, and thus appear disconnected from the Fall, seems hard to square with a creation that, from the start, is created good."[13] His discomfort lies in attributing natural evil to God instead of human sin, but he admits that this is what science appears to demonstrate: "If human sin no longer seems responsible for natural evil, that's because science has made it difficult to see how human sin could be responsible for natural evil."

To get out of this bind, Dembski proposes something quite novel: "We should understand the corrupting effects of the Fall also *retroactively* (in other words, the consequences of the Fall can also act backward into the past). Accordingly, the Fall could take place *after* the natural evils for which it is responsible."[14]

Dembski still believes in Adam, Eve, and the Garden of Eden (which he holds was safely sealed off from the fallen world that had been raging for billions of years). Even though Adam and Eve's act of disobedience in the Garden was a relatively recent act in history, the consequences of this act were built into creation from the beginning. This is not an easy scenario to comprehend, partly because it relies on the notion of God being outside of chronological time. So, as far as chronological time goes — the only kind of time we humans know — creation has always been home to natural evil. In other words, the world looks as if there was no such thing as the Fall. Yet Dembski argues that the world has always been this way *because* Adam and Eve would eventually pick the forbidden fruit in the Garden of Eden. He suggests a biblical precedent for this reasoning can be found in the Old Testament saints being saved by Jesus' sacrifice on the cross — an event that occurred centuries after the lives of the saints.[15]

This view as of yet hasn't gained much traction — probably

---

[13] William Dembski, *The End of Christianity* (Nashville: B&H Publishing, 2009), 48.

[14] Ibid., 50.

[15] Ibid., 50.

in large part because there's no reason to believe it's true. Dembski's theory admits that science has uncovered a world that shows no sign of a Fall. He has hypothesized a scenario that is totally unfalsifiable — a scenario which is indistinguishable from one in which Christianity is *not* true. Furthermore, this idea is not found in the Bible. Why would the Bible be so misleading? Did God, who purportedly inspired the Bible, want to confuse people? He had to know that once science progressed to a certain point, the accuracy and truth of his book would be seriously questioned. As even Dembski says, "Until the last two or three centuries, the first chapters of Genesis seemed to make perfect sense as both theology and history."[16] Young earth creationist Philip Bell criticizes Dembski for bending his theology to accommodate science: "Human ingenuity is a very poor substitute for faithful acceptance of God's Word . . . just the latest in a long line of examples of Christians failing to accept the authority of the Bible."[17]

Dembski openly acknowledges that young earth theology and biblical interpretation has been the "overwhelming consensus of theologians up through the Reformation." He adds, "I myself would adopt it in a heartbeat except that nature seems to present such strong evidence against it."[18] To Dembski's credit, he knows young earth creationism is simply no longer tenable, and saving Christianity will require some ingenuity.

I do admire his bold effort, but his proposed solution smacks of desperation, betraying the trouble Christianity is in.

ADAM AND EVE TRY TO FIT IN

Through the centuries Christians have managed to deal with other instances where the Bible clashes with science. When the Bible assumes the earth is flat, or the sun rotates around a

---

[16] Ibid., 34.

[17] Philip Bell, "The 'problem' of evil and the supremacy of Scripture," October 12, 2010 http://creation.com/end-of-christianity-review, (May 12, 2017).

[18] Dembski, 55.

stationary earth, or that stars are objects that can fall to the earth, Christians were able to reinterpret this language as "poetic."[19]

Why don't Christians just do the same with the early chapters of Genesis? Some do, but doctrines begin to fall like dominoes. As we've seen, the historicity of Adam, Eve, and the Fall has long been integral to Christian theology. Christianity was not built upon the Bible's understanding of the nature of stars, for example. It *was* built upon the idea that we live in a fallen world and are consequently in need of a savior. So how does the story of Adam, Eve, and the Fall mesh with a 4.5 billion year old earth?

One of the trickiest issues for old earth creationists is deciding when Adam and Eve lived. When did God create this first human couple? Given that the fossil record shows a gradual progression leading to modern humans, drawing a bright-line between "animals" and "humans" isn't easy, but it is theologically necessary. Adam and Eve were uniquely created bearing the image of God. (In RTB's model, Neanderthals and all other non-modern humans are considered animals.)[20]

In their book, *Who Was Adam?*, Hugh Ross and Fazale Rana (President and Vice President of Reasons To Believe) place the creation of the human race somewhere between 10,000 and 100,000 years ago.[21] While they keep this 90,000-year window open for some wiggle room, they do favor a date of between 40,000 and 50,000 years ago.[22] They argue for this date based on archaeological findings that demonstrate the emergence of human artistic expression, a sense of spirituality, and more sophisticated tools: "At around 40,000 years ago, the archaeological record reveals a sociocultural explosion. This 'big bang' of human culture consists of new behaviors that can be

---

[19] There are still a few geocentrists around.

[20] Fazale Rana and Hugh Ross, *Who Was Adam* (Colorado Springs: Navpress, 2005), 50.

[21] Ibid., 45.

[22] Ibid., 66, 80, 84-5, 95, 137.

taken to reflect the image of God."[23] They corroborate this date with some cherry-picked genetic and fossil evidence. Before getting into the merits of drawing a dividing line through this particular point of hominid history (humans on one side, animals on the other), let's just see how it fits with the Bible.

To move the creation date of Adam and Eve back farther than 6,000 years ago, old earth creationists must contend with the genealogies in Genesis that link Adam to Abraham. As supporters of an inerrant Bible, RTB maintains the traditional belief that these genealogies record actual history.[24] They accept, for example, the biblical claim that people used to live to be over 900 years old. Remember, these genealogies specify how long each patriarch lived as well as the age at which each patriarch fathered the next person on the list. But to move Adam and Eve back farther than 6,000 years ago, most old earth creationists suggest that there are gaps in the genealogies. In other words, the biblical authors purposely left out some generations. Because these genealogies are divided neatly into two groups of ten patriarchs each, some argue less important names were omitted to maintain this balanced structure. For example, Genesis 5.12 says, "Kenan lived seventy years, and became the father of Mahalalel." A supporter of this view would interpret this passage as Kenan, at 70 years old, having fathered the *family line* that eventually gave rise to Mahalalel, not necessarily Mahalalel himself.

Let's get back to Ross's and Rana's suggesting a start date for humanity of about 45,000 years ago. The average age between each generation in the Genesis genealogies is about 100 years (#olddads). This means the biblical authors would have left out about 390 generations from the list![25] This is a little hard to believe, especially given that other parts of the Bible reinforce an actual father-son relationship for some of the characters on the

---

[23] Ibid., 137.

[24] Ibid., 46-7, 50.

[25] 45,000 (Adam) - 4,000 (Abraham) = 41,000 years. Divide that by 100 and subtract the 20 generations provided in the text.

list. Seth, for example, is the actual son of Adam, and Enosh is the actual son of Seth (Gen. 4.25). Jude 14 explicitly confirms that Enoch was the seventh generation from Adam. Where would these hundreds of missing generations fit? Sometimes you just have to admit that the Bible means what it says . . . and it's wrong. If the genealogies were not intended to provide us with a timeline, but just a gap-ridden list of people, why did the author go out of his way to cite the age at which each man fathered the next person on the list? This would be a strange and irrelevant detail to include.

Smuggling some 390 missing generations into the text strains credibility, but it gets even worse. Scientifically, a start date of 45,000 years ago for humanity just doesn't work. In their ten year update to *Who Was Adam?*, Ross and Rana were forced to move Adam and Eve back to about 150,000 years ago![26]

Molecular anthropology has compellingly demonstrated genetic continuity between us and humans of at least 150,000 years ago. There's no credible way to separate us from them.

If you and I could trace our ancestry back far enough, eventually we'd find that we share a great great great . . . grandma. We would also find we share a distant grandpa. Scientists often refer to all living people's most recent common matrilineal ancestor as "Mitochondrial Eve" and our most recent common patrilineal ancestor as "Y-chromosomal Adam."

Most of our DNA — the DNA stashed in the nuclei of our cells — is a unique blend from our mother and father. Unlike this nuclear DNA, our mitochondrial DNA is given to us only from our mother. You inherited a copy of your mom's mitochondrial DNA. If you are a male, you will not pass on your mitochondrial DNA to your kids; they will get their copy from their mother. Similarly, all males inherited their Y chromosome from their father. Using genetic mutation rates, scientists can estimate how far back mitochondrial Eve and Y-chromosomal Adam lived. The establishment of deep, unbroken matrilineal

---

[26] Fazale Rana and Hugh Ross, Who Was Adam? (Covina, CA: RTB Press, 2015), 266.

and patrilineal lines has forced RTB to drastically push the Garden of Eden back in time.

The scientific consensus is clear that these are not the first two humans, just the *most recent* female and male to whom we're all related (i.e. Mitochondrial Eve had a mom, and her mom had a mom, and so on). Furthermore, there never was a single couple, but always a population of early humans.[27] In fact, these two ancient humans likely did not even live at the same time. But RTB is not dissuaded by these details. They interpret the data as pointing to the biblical Adam and Eve. The dating of mitochondrial Eve and Y-chromosomal Adam is not precise, but RTB realizes that roughly 150,000 years ago is the latest date to credibly put these two figures together. The truth is, they don't have a lot of options.

Let's assume that Y-chromosomal Adam and mitochondrial Eve were actually the first couple and that a date of 150,000 years ago is accurate. What happens to those genealogies? Forget about it! They've already been stretched beyond their breaking point.

There are other problems with this date. Homo Sapiens began their transition from hunter gatherers to settled agriculturers about 12,000 years ago. Yet Genesis 4 speaks of agriculture and cities as already existing in the days of Cain and Abel. Old earthers have to figure out why the Bible is talking about agriculture and cities being firmly in place around 150,000 years ago. (The obvious answer is that the Bible was written by people who had no idea about humanity's deep pre-agricultural history.)

The Bible also reports that this is when snakes began to slither on their bellies. "Now the serpent was more crafty than any beast of the field which the Lord God had made" (Gen. 3.1). One of these crafty snakes encouraged Eve to pick the forbidden fruit. Part of God's punishment for this "original sin" is then

---

[27] The mitochondrial DNA and Y chromosome of the contemporaries of mitochondrial Eve and Y-chromosomal Adam hit a dead end at some point due to only having sons, daughters, or nothing.

directed at snakes:

> Because you have done this, cursed are you more than all cattle, and more than every beast of the field; on your belly you will go, and dust you will eat all the days of your life; and I will put enmity between you and the woman, and between your seed and her seed; he shall bruise you on the head, and you shall bruise him on the heel (Gen. 3.14-15).

Because the snake in the Garden was complicit in Eve's disobedience, the thousands of species of snakes that exist today no longer enjoy the perk of legs, which used to elevate them above the dirt. (Having your face right at ground level really does seem undesirable.) Again, science is at odds with the Bible. Fossils of legless snakes date back millions of years.

This ancient story is obviously an etiological one, written by ancient people trying to explain the way things are. Why don't we like snakes? All the other land animals get legs, why don't they? This story provides answers. Ancient explanations of this type were common.

Another awkward byproduct of the old earth position concerns the creation of women:

> Then the Lord God said, "It is not good for the man to be alone; I will make him a helper suitable for him." Out of the ground the Lord God formed every beast of the field and every bird of the sky, and brought them to the man to see what he would call them; and whatever the man called a living creature, that was its name. The man gave names to all the cattle, and to the birds of the sky, and to every beast of the field, but for Adam there was not found a helper suitable for him. So the Lord God caused a deep sleep to fall upon the man, and he slept; then He took one of his ribs and closed up the flesh at that place. The Lord God fashioned into a woman the rib which He had taken from the man, and brought her to the man. The man said, "This is now bone of my bones, and flesh of my flesh; she shall be called Woman, because she was taken out of Man" (Gen. 2.18-23).

Adam is alone, God shows the animals to Adam, but he finds no suitable match. God then creates something new called a *woman*. I can see this story working for young earth creationists. But treating the idea of inventing a woman to be matched with a man as a novel concept just doesn't work in an old earth context. All the other early human species already had women. *Homo erectus*, *Homo heidelbergensis*, Neanderthals, Denisovans, and even "pre-Adam and Eve" *Homo sapiens* all had women. Women existed before 150,000 years ago, just as they existed after. The Bible knows nothing about earth's actual history.

BOTTOM LINE: THIS ISN'T BELIEVABLE

Adam and Eve's first disobedient act changed everything. We live in a fallen world because of it. Our consequent corrupted nature distances us from God and slates us all for hell. Jesus is the only way to restore what was broken and save us from damnation.

I wonder if the cavemen living 100,000 years ago knew anything about this grim predicament they were in. Of course not. Abraham and Moses didn't even know anything about it. Their contemporaries in China, Africa, Australia, the Americas, and everywhere else certainly were not aware of their desperate need for a savior. This seems like pretty important information. Would God not have been more forthcoming about such news? He certainly didn't seem to be in a big rush to patch things up after the Fall. 148,000 years strikes me as a long time to wait to tell all these poor hominids that they're on a highway to hell.

Then there's the problem of having no evidence of a Fall. Imposing a reality-changing, cosmic shift onto the long steady timeline of life on earth 150,000 years ago smells desperate and make-believe. We're supposed to believe we actually fell from a higher, idyllic state, while we know death, suffering, violence, and procreation have been with us before and after this date or any other date an apologist chooses.

Finally, this model just doesn't match up with Genesis. We'd have to believe that these cavemen had agriculture, cities, and Jewish names over 100,000 years ago. We'd have to believe that this is when snakes started slithering on their bellies. We'd have to make sense of the notion that this is when God first decided to create females, as if pairing a female with a male is some novel idea at this point in history. I honestly can't see how I could believe this, especially when it makes remarkably more sense to read these stories as ancient creation myths, which of course they are.

The Flood

Because scientists know the worldwide flood described in Genesis never happened, RTB advocates for a "geographically limited" flood. "The RTB model considers the extent of the flood to be 'universal' in that all humanity was impacted by it."[28] In other words, this was just a regional flood, but God did indeed drown every single person, except for Noah, his wife, his three sons, and their wives. This interpretation is dubious both scripturally and scientifically. Moral of the story: If your starting point is that the Bible is the perfect word of God, you'll get tied in knots trying to make it so.

---

[28] Fazale Rana and Hugh Ross, *Who Was Adam?* (Covina, CA: RTB Press, 2015), 54-5.

4. ADJUSTING FOR EVOLUTION

Old earth creationists have tried to shed the most scientifically embarrassing parts of young earth creationism, often at the expense of scripture, but their embrace of science is far from complete. The war on evolution, especially human evolution, has been waged by young and old earth creationists alike. By rejecting evolution, Christians preserve the inerrancy of the Bible, God's agency as a designer, and a specially created first human couple who brought sin and death into the world, resulting in the need for a savior.

While evolution is still majorly scorned by many evangelical Christians, some are making the case that it's time to make peace. Evolution is here to stay. Whether we like it or not, those are our distant cousins we're visiting at the zoo.

It's time to introduce our third "creationist" camp. Meet *evolutionary creationism* (aka *theistic evolution*). Evolutionary creationists believe the God of the Bible chose to create human beings through the process of biological evolution. Francis Collins, who directed the Human Genome Project and currently heads the National Institutes of Health, has been instrumental in recent efforts to bring evolution and Christianity together. Besides being a high-profile scientist, Collins is a committed evangelical Christian. As director of the Human Genome Project, he knows better than anyone that denying evolution is no longer an option for Christians. He states, "The predictions of evolution have been borne out in more ways than Darwin could have possibly imagined."[1]

To promote, defend, and develop evolutionary creationism, Collins founded the Biologos Foundation, launching their public website (biologos.org) in 2009. Since then, the foundation has played an integral role in expanding the acceptance of evolution within Christendom. While this relatively new camp still faces fierce opposition from within their own evangelical ranks, the needle is definitely moving.

CAN THESE TWO WORLDVIEWS BECOME ONE?

God chose to bring about humans through a 14 billion year process. Millions of species would suffer, die, and go extinct, but eventually God's chosen species would emerge. This would be a curious process to employ if One's purpose is to create human beings, but evolutionary creationist Dr. Denis Alexander nonetheless tries to spin it as a positive. "We could so easily have gone extinct like the Neanderthals, and it is a sign of God's loving sovereign plan and purposes for humankind that we were preserved."[2] By that logic, God must adore horseshoe crabs, which have avoided extinction since well before the dinosaurs!

When God's creative work is hidden behind seemingly natural processes a question arises. Isn't a natural explanation sufficient? On a Christian debate podcast, scientist Robert Stovold employed a "cornflakes" metaphor to demonstrate evolution's effect on the design argument (read with English accent for maximum impact):

If you see lots of small cornflakes in the bottom of a cornflakes

---

[1] Kathryn Applegate and J. B. Stump, eds., *How I Changed My Mind About Evolution* (Downers Grove, IL: InterVarsity Press, 2016), 71-2.

[2] Denis Alexander, Creation or Evolution: *Do We Have To Choose?* (Oxford: Monarch Books, 2014), 265.

packet and you know that small flakes can fall through large gaps and large flakes can't fall through small gaps, and you see the small flakes on the bottom of the packet — it says on the packet "contents may have settled in transit." Now there are perfectly natural explanations for why the small flakes are at the bottom. If a theistic evolutionist says 'well I know it looks like the flakes got there through random natural vibrations of the cornflakes packet... but actually they got there because God put them there' — now I can't disprove that but it seems to me incredibly contrived.[3]

Bible scholars Robert Price and Edwin Suominen smell something fishy too: The "process of natural selection is *inherently* blind and aimless, random, hit-and-miss. If that is not so, and if there is some Entity guiding the process, why is it not evident?"[4] Is this stealth God of evolution the same God who parted the Red Sea, who smote the firstborn in Egypt, or who caused the sun and moon to stand still? I think I can at least show that it's not the same God who inspired the book of Genesis.

Mapping evolution onto the Christian story will require even more ingenuity than did old earth creationism. President of the Southern Baptist Theological Seminary Albert Mohler reminds us that "If there is no historical Adam, then the Bible's metanarrative is not Creation-Fall-Redemption-New Creation but something very different." Can Adam survive evolution?

Christianity tells us that humans fell from a higher state, not that they evolved from wild animals. Remember, our tainted nature — that darn propensity to do the wrong thing — was not part of God's original design. Adam and Eve were created in a state of righteousness, innocence and harmony with God, but nonetheless managed to disobey him. They were expelled from an idyllic garden, saddled with a fallen nature, and every one of us now stands unavoidably guilty before God. Only Jesus'

---

[3] Robert Stovold on *Unbelievable?*, Podcast audio, June 21, 2008.

[4] Robert M. Price and Edwin A. Suominen, *Evolving out of Eden* (Valley, WA: Tellectual Press, 2013), 269.

atoning death can restore this broken relationship. (The traditional story has problems of its own: God's original design couldn't have been *that* good if the very first generation went awry.)

So, Christianity maintains that we have fallen from our loftier, originally intended nature. But if in reality, we're actually emerging from wild animalhood, there's a big problem. It's no wonder the main forces of opposition to evolution are Christian.

EVOLUTION + CHRISTIANITY: NOT A MATCH MADE IN HEAVEN

There's a common perception that we live in especially horrible times. Terrorism, gang violence, campus rape, hate crimes, unsavory video games, pornography, punk-ass kids — human depravity seems to get worse every day. There's no denying the suffering and the immense challenges we face today, but we also need to put our modern world in perspective. Our past is not pretty. Human sacrifice, animal sacrifice, witch hunts, torture, slavery, and misogyny — we look back at our ancestors' barbaric and unenlightened practices with bewilderment and disgust.

Cognitive scientist Steven Pinker speaks of the "escalator of reason," which over time has lifted the moral standards of the human race. We've slowly figured out that there are rational reasons to behave better. It hasn't been a smooth ascent, but the trajectory is clear. Over the millennia we've made significant moral progress. Understandably, you're probably a bit skeptical of this assertion. After all, violence, racism, sexism, and even torture and slavery in some form still exist today. But with a few examples I think I can illuminate the chasm between our moral standards and those of our ancestors. Brace yourself.

On *Dan Carlin's Hardcore History* podcast, Carlin recounts a story from 16th century Europe, when the Reformation had cracked open western Christendom.[5] A new sect known as

---

[5] Dan Carlin "Prophets of Doom," *Dan Carlin's Hardcore History*, Podcast audio, April 22, 2013.

Anabaptists had taken control of the German city of Münster and established a fanatical community under the cultish leadership of a man named Jan Van Leiden. When the Prince-Bishop's forces finally took back Münster, Van Leiden and two of his co-conspirators were captured and sentenced to death.

Back then, the authorities weren't necessarily interested in administering quick deaths. Van Leiden's execution was staged in the city center where crowds of people gathered to watch the show. After the charges had been read, the executioners began to tear off chunks of his flesh with glowing-hot iron tongs. Starting with his armpits, they proceeded to remove skin, muscles, tendons, and his tongue. Van Leiden wasn't allowed to die until he had suffered a full hour of hot tong flesh removal. If he passed out, his time was paused until he was revived.

Compare this ghastly event to capital punishment today. In the United States, which is now unique among western countries for even having a death penalty, no one is debating whether or not hot-tong-flesh-removal events in public squares are too barbaric. Instead, the debate centers on whether lethal injection is too barbaric. There's quite a difference between a culture that strives to maximize the pain of execution and one that tries to minimize it, if not eliminate execution altogether.

To be fair, not everyone tried to maximize the pain of execution in 16th century Europe. The very same year that Jan Van Leiden was executed, Henry VIII "mercifully" arranged for his wife, Anne Boleyn, to be beheaded rather than burned alive. As if this weren't merciful enough, King Henry replaced the common axe-wielding executioner with a skilled swordsman.

For some reason the awfulness of stories from the distant past tend to lose some of their sting. So just for good measure, imagine Prince William ordering the beheading of Kate Middleton outside Buckingham Palace in London today.

But what about ISIS? Yeah. We don't all climb the escalator of reason in lockstep. Yet, in a different century, their brutality and blasphemy laws wouldn't warrant any special attention at all. The fact that ISIS shocks our modern sensibilities is a testament to our general rise up the escalator.

Practices that are flagrantly immoral to us today were apparently not so to our ancestors. Women weren't even guaranteed the right to vote in the United States until 1920. That's a mere 100 years ago! What might the status of women have looked like a few millennia ago? Pinker offers us a glimpse from Homeric Greece: "The 21st century has certainly seen the rape of women in wartime, but it has long been treated as an atrocious war crime, which most armies try to prevent and the rest deny and conceal. But for the heroes of the *Iliad*, female flesh was a legitimate spoil of war."[6] Sadly, this stance is echoed in the Bible. "When the Lord your God gives it into your hand, you shall strike all the men in it with the edge of the sword. Only the women and the children and the animals and all that is in the city, all its spoil, you shall take as booty for yourself; and you shall use the spoil of your enemies which the Lord your God has given you" (Deut. 20.13-14). "Kill every male among the little ones, and kill every woman who has known man intimately. But all the girls who have not known man intimately, spare for yourselves" (Num. 31.17-18).

War is inherently ugly, but the *Iliad* and the Bible still manage to expose the exceptional savagery of ancient thinking: "We are not going to leave a single one of them alive, down to the babies in their mothers' wombs — not even they must live."[7] "They will fall by the sword, their little ones will be dashed in pieces, and their pregnant women will be ripped open."[8]

Can you imagine if these ancient cultures had machine guns, nukes, and social media? You think your Facebook feed is depressing now? Don't get me wrong, people commit heinous acts of cruelty and stupidity every day, but let's keep our nostalgia in check. Sure, we might watch our share of violence in movies, but in real life cat-burning, bearbaiting, and burning women at the stake for alleged witchcraft are no longer socially acceptable.

---

[6] Steven Pinker, *The Better Angels of Our Nature* (New York: Penguin, 2011), 5.

[7] Homer *Iliad* quoted from Pinker, 4.

[8] The Bible, Hosea 13.16

Even with today's modern weaponry, warfare, and terrorism, the chances of your dying a violent death have dropped drastically over the last 10,000 years. Slavery, once a universally accepted practice, is illegal around the globe. Rights for women and racial minorities have improved tremendously. We're currently witnessing the decriminalization of homosexuality and the legalization of same-sex marriage at an unprecedented pace. Children are now treated better. We're learning to treat animals better. The expansion of our circle of empathy is undeniable.[9] To recap, we haven't fallen down, we're climbing up.

A second point is that evolution seems a rather peculiar method for God to choose if he's going to hold *Homo sapiens* to such high standards. We see our tribal tendencies mirrored in other species. Chimpanzees, with whom we share a relatively recent ancestor, mercilessly attack other chimps who belong to neighboring communities. These attacks are almost always committed by males. By picking off other males, chimps compete to increase "their access to resources such as food and mates."[10] Pinker offers details of chimp violence: "If they encounter a solitary male, or isolate one from a small group, they will go after him with murderous savagery. Two attackers will hold down the victim, and the others will beat him, bite off his toes and genitals, tear flesh from his body, twist his limbs, drink his blood, or rip out his trachea."[11]

Would God really use natural selection to bring about humans and then damn them to hell for being the way they are? If God is so disappointed with the results, maybe he should have used a different method.

Evolution paints an entirely different picture of humanity from the one assumed in Christian theology. The truth is we're

---

[9] Pinker uses the term "expanding circle" but attributes to Peter Singer, 175, 648.

[10] Michael L. Wilson et al., "Lethal aggression in Pan is better explained by adaptive strategies than human impacts," Nature, September 17, 2014, http://www.nature.com/nature/journal/v513/n7518/full/nature13727.html.

[11] Pinker, 37.

not fallen. Everything is as one would expect given our evolutionary past. If nothing broke, if there was no original sin or Fall, Christians need to rewrite the reasoning behind Jesus' crucifixion. What purpose did it serve? And why are members of the *Homo sapiens* species allegedly so guilty that they deserve eternal punishment? I guess what I'm trying to say is if God is going to opt for a creative process in which activities such as kickin' ass and havin' lots of sex help to get your genes passed on, he's going to get what he paid for. Or, even more articulately stated by Price and Suominen, "Those actions that have been labeled as 'sin' do not arise from any subsequent corruption of our nature, but *from our very nature itself* as the descendants of reproductive survivors in a harsh and brutal world."[12]

HOW DO WE START THIS STORY?

So how would one go about reconstructing the Christian narrative in light of evolution? First, one needs a starting point. When were the first humans? Uhhh. Evolution is a slow gradual process, so locating the first humans in history is nonsensical. The belief in a first couple must be scrapped. The theologian must instead posit a time in history when God inaugurated a relationship with two humans named Adam and Eve, who subsequently disobeyed him. Theologically, the question at hand is, at what point in history did *Homo sapiens* become guilty before God and need saving?

Genesis 1.27 reads, "God created man in His own image, in the image of God He created him; male and female He created them." The image of God apparently makes us unique amongst the animals. The biblical authors were referring to the actual creation of the first humans, but since evolution precludes a genetic starting point for the human race, many evolutionary creationists suggest that the text must be referring to a point in history when God injected already-existing humans with his image. But given that humans evolved gradually, both

---

[12] Price and Suominen, 190.

biologically and culturally, this is also a troubled notion. Was there such a species-changing event? When? How far back should we go in the gradual and continuous process of human evolution?

One of the most well-known fossils is from a hairy little lady, dubbed Lucy, who lived about three million years ago. Did Lucy need a savior? I'm sure that little sinner at least stole a piece of fruit once. How about *Homo erectus*? This human species had a pretty good run. They were quite handy with stone tools, spread across multiple continents, and inhabited the earth for well over a million years. Did their souls need saving? Maybe the program started about 200,000 years ago, when anatomically modern humans began to emerge. Perhaps God's image was infused 40,000 years ago, when humans were showcasing their artistic flair (although scientists are uncovering artistic inclinations from well before this date). Genesis mentions cities and agriculture around the time of Adam and Eve; maybe God stepped in about 8,000 years ago when agricultural societies began to form.

Any starting point one chooses quickly feels arbitrary and uncomfortable. Evolutionary creationists don't claim to know for sure when God stamped his image on humans or when they fell; they just know it happened. But when it happened is a mystery. Very mysterious indeed.

Despite the fact that evolution rules out the biblical notion of there being a first man and woman from whom we all descend, most evolutionary creationists still regard Adam and Eve as real people. They attempt to retain their historicity for a couple reasons. The biblical authors, who were supposed to be inspired by God, consistently demonstrate their belief that Adam and Eve were historical people. In the New Testament we read, "For it was Adam who was first created, and then Eve. And it was not Adam who was deceived, but the woman being deceived, fell into transgression" (1 Tim. 2.13-14). In multiple genealogies, the authors link real people back to Adam. The Gospel of Luke connects Jesus' lineage back to Adam. Paul, who is responsible for much of Christianity as we know it, refers to the time between Adam and Moses (Rom. 5.14), implying this was an actual span of time in history. Jesus refers to the "days of Noah," implying Noah was real too. Not many biblical scholars will contest that the biblical writers believed Adam and Eve were real people. Could the "inspired" authors have been wrong? And secondly, can the Christian storyline be kept intact without a historical Adam and Eve? These challenges compel many evolutionary creationists to keep them around.

TRYING TO FIND ADAM AND EVE A COMFORTABLE HOME

Given that there never was a time when a single human couple existed, evolutionary creationists often view Adam and Eve as God's chosen couple amongst the human population. What might this look like? Let's look at some possibilities.

EARLY MODERN HUMANS

One option is that Adam and Eve lived in Africa around 200,000 years ago, when anatomically modern humans surfaced. Even though this scenario places the couple early in *Homo sapiens* history, proponents are still forced to abandon the traditional belief that all people descend from Adam and Eve for the simple reason that there would have been about 10,000 other people living at the same time. Old Testament professor C. John Collins argues that *if* one were to stretch the Genesis story to allow for a population of early humans, "he or she should envision these humans as a single tribe of closely related members. Adam would then be the chieftain of this tribe."[13] The picture that emerges is so far removed from the biblical story that one has to wonder why anybody is even bothering to recreate it, but let's try.

200,000 years ago, various human species were in existence. One of them, *Homo sapiens*, living in Africa at the time, was the object of God's creation. God established a line of

---

[13] Matthew Barrett and Ardel B. Caneday, eds., *Four Views on the Historical Adam* (Grand Rapids: Zondervan, 2013), 171-2.

communication with their chieftain and his wife, Adam and Eve. This band of hominids, who were pretty good at using stone tools and possibly fire, enjoyed a close relationship with God. But this relationship didn't last long. Adam and Eve went astray, causing the fall of the human race.

Supporters of this model would need to figure out what this means. Did anything change? (Every subsequent human would now deserve to go to hell, of course, but was there any noticeable change in the observable universe?) Christianity has always held that this is the point at which death was introduced to the human experience. A report commissioned by the Evangelical Alliance affirms that "Our mortality is a consequence of sin, which in turn derives from humanity's original rebellion against God."[14] But death is a key ingredient of the evolutionary process. It did not originate with Adam and Eve's sin. Humans and other animals have always died. Therefore most evolutionary creationists drop the traditional position and settle for "spiritual" death, which refers to a broken relationship with God. For a very brief moment, 200,000 years ago, primitive people knew the God of the Bible, but then died (spiritually). Because Adam, the chieftain from 200,000 years ago, was the spiritual representative of the human race, we're now all born with a fallen nature that separates us from God and inevitably leads us into sin.

Evolutionary creationists are attempting to repackage the Fall in a way that doesn't conflict with reality. They're searching for a quiet, imperceptible, unfalsifiable Fall (whether it is believable seems secondary). But they still have to figure out if, as the Bible says, God greatly multiplied the pain of childbirth as a result of Eve's disobedience, or cursed the ground, making agriculture (which, by the way, didn't exist 200,000 years ago) much more difficult because of Adam's sin.

The story then picks up again 198,000 years after this alleged Fall, when God notifies some humans in a remote corner

---

[14] Evangelical Alliance Commission on Unity and Truth Among Evangelicals, *The Nature of Hell* (London: Acute, 2000), 130.

of the earth that they need a savior because some ancient hominid disobeyed him 198,000 years ago. Is it just me, or is this an example of bending over backwards trying to squeeze history from an ancient creation myth?

NEOLITHIC FARMERS

Let's be honest, when the authors of Genesis wrote the story of Adam and Eve, they were not describing two (out of many) primitive people who lived 200,000 years ago. Another attempt at harmonizing the text with reality is to hypothesize that Adam and Eve were neolithic farmers living within the last 8,000 years or so. Denis Alexander, former director of the Faraday Institute for Science and Religion, holds to this scenario, at least "until a better one comes along,"[15] partly because it "locates these events within the culture and geography that the Genesis text provides."[16] That is, this more recent date recovers some of the scriptural advantages enjoyed by young earth creationists. For example, the Genesis text refers to farming and cities, which were developing around this time. This tighter timeframe can also put the genealogies that link Adam and Abraham back in play. Additionally, the Bible places Adam and Eve near the Tigris and Euphrates rivers, not in Africa where *Homo sapiens* started. Eight thousand years ago, people had long left Africa and were spread around the globe, so adherents of this model are free to repatriate Adam and Eve back to the Middle East.

But as evolutionary creationists try to align bits of Genesis with history, one could accuse them of cherry-picking. For example, are they willing to affirm that people, such as Adam the neolithic farmer, used to live to be 900 years old as the Bible claims? I doubt it. Doing so would defeat the whole purpose of fitting the story into reality. But to be credible, they need to be consistent, not opportunistic in their interpretations.

Let's try to flesh out this scenario. Critical thinking, artistic

---

[15] Alexander, 358.

[16] Ibid., 290.

expression, spiritual beliefs — the hallmarks of what Christians would term the "image of God" — were well established in humans long before 8,000 years ago. So the idea that this is when God stamped humans with his image doesn't work. Humans were human before and after 8,000 years ago. They didn't go to bed one night as wild animals and wake up as artists and poets.

Perhaps the image of God "evolved." Maybe what we thought were the processes of biological and cultural evolution were actually God slowly stamping humans with his image. Smuggling God into ostensibly natural processes affords the believer some protection. This hypothesis is impossible to falsify but it's theologically awkward. During this long process of God gradually releasing his image into humanity, were there humans (animals?) with only half an image of God, or a 1/16, or a whatever? Did some fraction of their soul need saving?

Evolutionary creationists can't agree on how or when humans received the image of God, they just know it happened. As Alexander asserts, "No one is in any doubt that it must have happened at some stage in history, but when exactly is not that important."[17] Hold on a second. If you can't find a believable place to put it, maybe you shouldn't presuppose it. You don't get to take for granted the very article of faith that you are trying to reestablish. The existence of a divide between image-of-God humans and non-image-of-God humans or between pre-Fall and post-Fall human history is exactly what evolution calls into question.

Back to the scenario at hand. God chooses some couple on planet Earth to be Adam and Eve. Adam is designated as the spiritual representative of every human on earth. God, Adam, and Eve (and maybe their entire farming community) are living in harmony, until the couple goes astray (whether this first sin was picking fruit from a forbidden tree or something else, we do not know). BOOM! The human race falls. People on far away continents instantly become sinners in the eyes of God because of what this farmer named Adam did. Aboriginal Australians,

---

[17] Ibid., 296.

for example, who had been developing their own religious beliefs, creation stories, and culture in isolation for 40,000 years have no idea what just happened. Did they think to themselves, *Is it just me, or is childbirth WAY more painful than it used to be?* Were women all of a sudden ruled over by their husbands? Did snakes instantly lose their legs? Did farming inexplicably become a difficult chore (Gen. 3.14-19)?[18] Of course not. Life went on — at least as far as they could tell. Little did they know, a couple farmers in a distant land just brought about their spiritual death! But no one would inform Aboriginal Australians of their spiritual death and dire need for a savior until thousands of years later when the British dumped their first load of convicts onto their continent.

CAN IT BE DONE?

Trying to fit evolutionary science into Christian theology is a daunting task. Some anti-evolution Christians say it's "like being on a mission to draw a round square."[19] I can see their point. But the image that comes to my mind is of a person who gains 100 pounds and then tries to fit back into their old jeans (think skinny jeans). No matter how emotionally attached one is to those jeans, it's not going to work — or at least it won't be pretty. The circumstances have changed.

WHAT IF THE BIBLE IS WRONG? NAH, THAT'S IMPOSSIBLE.

There is a glaring weakness at the base of the entire

---

[18] If the curses of Genesis 3 didn't happen, how should the believer interpret these passages? Are they conveying some deeper truth? Are they metaphorically describing other consequences that are conveniently unfalsifiable? Any alternative interpretation must make more sense than an etiological one. Genesis 3 was written by ancient people trying to make sense of their world. Why is giving birth so painful? Why would God create thorns and thistles? Why are snakes freaky? Why don't they get legs like the other land animals?

[19] Cameron Buettel, "Evangelical Syncretism: The Genesis Crisis," February 17, 2015, https://www.gty.org/library/blog/B150217/evangelical-syncretism-the-genesis-crisis, (May 18, 2017).

evolutionary creationist enterprise. All the smart, capable, credentialed scholars are working and building upon a massive assumption that there can be no conflict between the Bible and science because "all knowledge is God's knowledge." Throughout their literature one finds reference to the two books: the book of scripture and the book of nature, God's word and God's world. "Ultimately, they cannot contradict each other because the source of both is the same God and if they seem to be in contradiction it is because we have misread one or both of them, and we need to be willing therefore to allow ourselves to be open to thinking about either one in different ways, trusting that God will ultimately lead us to see the truth of the whole."[20] No matter how far off from reality the Bible appears, the possibility that it is wrong is not an option. The Bible is the inspired word of God, period.

Encouraging Christians to not fear science, Francis Collins asks, "If God created the universe and the laws that govern it, and if he endowed human beings with intellectual abilities to discern its workings, would he want us to disregard those abilities? Would he be diminished or threatened by what we are discovering about his creation?"[21] I don't think so, but the Bible might be "diminished or threatened." The fact that science could expose the Bible as a wholly uninspired book doesn't seem to occur to Collins and friends. Fuller Theological Seminary professor Oliver D. Crisp perpetuates this flawed approach. "We begin from a position of faith, and seek to understand what we are committed to."[22] This thinking leads to what I call *backwards scholarship* (starting with a conclusion and then figuring out how to defend it). Crisp goes on, "If evolution is true, and all truth is God's truth, and faith seeks understanding . . . then evolution and biblical Christianity must in principle be consonant with one

---

[20] Mark H. Mann, "Augustine of Hippo and Two Books Theology, Part 2," January 5, 2015, http://biologos.org/blogs/archive/augustine-of-hippo-and-two-books-theology-part-2, (May 18, 2017).

[21] Applegate and Stump, 73.

[22] Ibid., 75.

another even if it sometimes appears that they are in conflict."[23] Well, if they don't appear to be consonant, then maybe biblical Christianity is wrong. Precluding this possibility is to willfully wear blinders.

The divine inspiration behind the Bible is not questioned by these theologians. The problem is always one of human interpretation. Pastor, author, and evolutionary creationist Richard Dahlstrom says, "With respect to the Bible, humility is important because history shows us how easy it is repeatedly to get our interpretations wrong — including the justification of slavery, colonialism and genocide."[24] Yeah, it's interesting how the "correct" interpretations surface once the old ones have been deemed unreasonable by modern science or society. Those passages about slavery or the second class status of women were curiously misinterpreted prior to the Civil War and prior to women's winning equal rights. Coincidentally, after these events, the correct interpretations became clear. Currently, Christians seem to be in the process of realizing that the Bible is not actually anti-gay. Old Testament scholar James Barr explained, "Inerrancy is maintained only by constantly altering the mode of interpretation, and in particular by abandoning the literal sense as soon as it would be an embarrassment."[25] Barr wrote this in 1977, but the trend continues as believers disavow literal interpretations of much of Genesis in order to preserve belief in an authoritative Bible.

Driven by the belief that the Bible and the book of nature cannot conflict, evolutionary creationists reject a straightforward reading of the early chapters of Genesis (most will claim the more pure kind of history kicks in after chapter 11). Despite rejecting a literal interpretation, the evolutionary creationism we've looked at thus far still can't help but try to repackage the story of Adam and Eve in the wrappings of evolution. What

---

[23] Ibid., 79.

[24] Ibid., 177.

[25] James Barr, *Fundamentalism* (Philadelphia: Westminster Press, 1978), 46.

results is some tortured combination of the biblical story and reality which shouldn't be satisfying to anyone.

ONE LAST STOP

There's one last stop on the evangelical train worth visiting. Some evolutionary creationists believe that seeking *concordance*, or agreement, between the early chapters of Genesis and actual historical events and people is a dead end. These *non-concordists* make a clean break with the ancient scientific and historical claims of the Bible. By admitting that the biblical writers brought ancient (and wrong) understandings of science and history into the Bible, they spare themselves of the pain of historicizing such things as the genealogies or Noah's Flood. Accordingly, they conclude that there was no Adam and Eve. Even though the biblical authors and subsequent Christian orthodoxy believed in and relied on their historicity, they were mistaken.

Denis Lamoureux, one of the leading voices of this position, does not come to it lightly: "Throughout history Christians have steadfastly believed that the creation of Adam from the dust of the ground in Genesis 2.7 refers to a real historical event. They have also held firmly to the notion that all humans have descended from Adam."[26] He also grants that the assumption that the Bible and science should align is "reasonable" and a "logical expectation" for Christians.[27] But alas, modern scholarship has shown that this is not the case.

Surprisingly, Lamoureux has no intention of abandoning the belief that the Bible is a divinely inspired book: "When the Holy Spirit inspired the biblical authors, He allowed them to use some of their ancient ideas about nature."[28] Divine inspiration isn't questioned. Because there are wrong ideas in the Bible, the Holy Spirit *must* have been OK with it.

To the discomfort of many Christians, Lamoureux then

---

[26] Barrett and Caneday, 57.

[27] Ibid., 45.

[28] Ibid., 41.

boldly demonstrates that the cosmology depicted in the Bible mirrors the "science-of-the-day" in the ancient Near East (i.e. it's wrong). The biblical worldview asserts there is a firmament, a huge dome that separates and holds up a sea of water up above. The Bible attests to a 3-tier universe in which heaven is located above the firmament and an underworld sits below the earth. The scriptures report a worldwide flood that swept the earth clean. The Bible speaks of stars which can be dislodged from the firmament and fall down to earth. "How can stars fall to earth when only one would destroy it completely? Understood from an ancient phenomenological perspective, this passage makes perfect sense. Stars look like tiny specks."[29]

For Lamoureux, the prevalence of what he terms "ancient science" in the Bible must be factored into our understanding of Adam. "No one today believes in a firmament, a heavenly sea, a 3-tier universe, or a geocentric world. Nor should we then believe in the historicity of Adam, and as a consequence, the doctrine of original sin."[30] That is, the Bible is wrong on all these points, and the doctrine of original sin is wrong too. This is a courageous move on Lamoureux's part, but he knows the survival of Christianity is at stake.

Proponents of this position hold that God used/allowed ancient misconceptions to deliver inerrant spiritual truths. "Whether birds were created before humans (Genesis 1) or after the man and before the woman (Genesis 2) is ultimately incidental and not essential to our personal relationship with the Lord," says Lamoureux.[31] God accommodated the Bible's original audience by coming down to their level and allowing their mistaken ideas to be canonized. Modern people must do their best to disentangle the inerrant message from its errant vessel. But there are a few problems.

If the Bible is wrong on so many verifiable points, why

---

[29] Ibid., 60.

[30] Denis O. Lamoureux, "Beyond Original Sin: Is a Theological Paradigm Shift Inevitable?" *Perspectives on Science and Christian Faith* 67, no. 1 (March 2015): 46.

[31] Ibid., 39.

should we trust that the unverifiable parts are true? Why believe a book filled with so many ancient misconceptions is inspired in the first place? If God decided to use ancient notions of cosmology and human origins, did he also opt for ancient morality? When the Bible speaks of females as war booty and war spoil, was God just trying to relate to his unenlightened, immediate audience? If the morality of the Bible is archaic, should, for instance, modern Christians base their moral opposition to same-sex marriage on this book? Are the biblical descriptions of God accurate, or are they just accommodations? Ancient gods needed blood sacrifices, changed their minds, and punished people through war and natural disaster, just like the God of the Bible does. How does the modern reader know what is true and what is the result of accommodation? No one is asking God to explain the intricacies of modern science to the ancients, but he could at least give them a dumbed down version of what actually happened, rather than a false version that would sow division, confusion, and unbelief in the future.

Additionally, can the ancient science be reliably separated from the "inerrant" theology? Christianity has been wrong about the reason for the universality of sin, death, and the need for a savior, but, Lamoureux would argue, that doesn't nullify the fact that sin, death, and the need for a savior are still real. It is true that people die and people do wrong, but the problem is that it was the purported *cause* of death and sin that justified the subsequent need for Jesus' sacrificial death. Jesus came to undo what Adam did. The theology wasn't merely conflated with the ancient science, it was based upon it.

Without original sin (and an original sinner), Christianity goes something like this: God chose to forge humans over millions of years through the harshest, most uncaring contest of survival. This process naturally produced imperfect beings. Nonetheless, God decided every single one of them deserves damnation for being as they are. The traditional story was already troubling, but at least there was a Fall, a rupture, caused by sinful humans. Something broke and Jesus came to fix it. But in this new model Lamoureux is stuck with a perfect God who created flawed creatures and then damned them to hell for being flawed. Replacing the front half of the Christian story with evolution while maintaining the traditional punchline makes for disjointed, uncompelling, and awkward theology. As Price and Suominen say, "What they do not seem to see is that the death of Jesus cannot be understood as a solution unless there is a prior problem to solve. And evolution replaces the whole Adam 'problem' with a scientific explanation."[32]

When such a foundational part of the story has been debunked, why keep what's left? The "spiritual truth" that's left, no longer fits the context. And perhaps the spiritual truth deserves the same scrutiny as the ancient science from which it is extracted. Might the concept of appeasing a deity through the shedding of blood also qualify as ancient thinking? Is this "spiritual truth" actually just ancient theology? And couldn't the belief that death entered the world as a result of sin, which Lamoureux dismisses as ancient science, also be categorized as a spiritual truth? These lines can be too easily gerrymandered.

Even though adherents of this model have freed themselves from the chore of historicizing Adam and Eve, they still must posit a point in history in which God started the you-need-a-savior program. At what point in the steady course of human development did God covertly flip the switch, making humans guilty for being human? With no sign of a Fall or earthly disruption, God's sudden initiation of the you-need-a-savior program must have happened secretly, behind the scenes, unbeknownst to the affected people down on earth.[33] *Before* this moment, when humans died, they would simply cease to exist,

---

[32] Price and Suominen, 187.

[33] I suppose one could alternatively hypothesize a moment in history in which God broke through to introduce himself and articulate his expectations to every human on the planet (perhaps like an emergency broadcast system). After this encounter, each individual made a conscious decision to disregard God's expectations in some way, which severed this relationship (not only for their own generation, but for all future humans). Everybody then resumed living just as they had always lived. I'm not sure if any or many believers subscribe to such a position, but this would be another example of straining to historicize the very story they're claiming is not historical.

just as when any other animal dies. But *after* this moment, damnation awaited these poor hominids (talk about being born in the wrong era).

Let's revisit Rick Warren's quote from chapter 1 to take stock of how far we've moved.

> How did God let everything get messed up? It started with Adam. . . . Adam's sin became our sin — all of us. That sin has laid comprehensive and awful consequences upon humanity. For example, it has led to natural disasters and deformities. Nature doesn't act like it should. It often acts irrationally, complete with hurricanes, tornadoes, earthquakes, and planet-disrupting menaces.[34]

Fast forward to our current model. There is no Adam and the world has always been this way. NOTHING changed. It's a last-ditch effort to salvage at least the semblance of orthodoxy. It's also an attempt to refashion Christianity as an entirely unfalsifiable religion. In fact, a world in which this new Christianity is true would appear indistinguishable from a world in which it is false.

ADAM AND EVE REMAIN HOMELESS

Price and Suomenin offer this astute observation: "Religion originally provided the explanation, but now it is what requires so much explaining."[35] Amen. The Bible no longer believably explains reality. Instead Christians continue to whittle down the literality of the Bible in search of a reading that can coexist with reality. But the fact that no one has been able to proffer a convincing, unifying solution to the disrupting forces of science is telling. Young earth creationists and evolutionary creationists are living on different planets. Even within evolutionary creationism, the plethora of views and lack of consensus is

---

[34] Rick Warren, "How Did We Get So Messed Up,
"http://pastorrick.com/devotional/english/how-did-we-get-so-messed-up,
[35] Price and Suominen., 314.

evidence of the trouble they're in. You can have a thousand proposals but if they're all bad it doesn't matter.

The bottom line is that the Christian worldview wasn't meant to handle evolution. And it should be no surprise that Christians have fiercely opposed it. Jesus warned of the incompatibility of putting new wine in old wineskins (Matt. 9.17), which is ironically fitting of what Christian evolutionists are trying to do. The fact that humans do bad things is not the same thing as humans being in a fallen state. There is no lost state of harmony. Death, murder, theft, jerks, birth defects, and earthquakes have always been around. There was no point in human history when any of this began. There was no original sin, original sinner, Fall or corruption of our nature. The history of *Homo sapiens* is as one would expect if Christianity isn't true. Unavoidably needing to be saved for being the result of a natural process is bizarre. And things get *really* weird when the punishment for being as we are is hell, where human souls are kept alive for eternity in never-ending misery.

5. GO TO HELL INFIDEL

Christianity holds that human beings are destined for one of two possible fates. As the Evangelical Free Church of America explains, "God will raise the dead bodily and judge the world, assigning the unbeliever to condemnation and eternal conscious punishment and the believer to eternal blessedness and joy."[1]

Let's meditate on this term "eternal conscious punishment" (aka eternal conscious torment). The non-Christian's punishment never ends. And we're not talking simply about a punishment that has eternal consequences (like you die and never come back). We're talking about consciously enduring utter misery forever and ever. After 100 trillion years of pure agony, your sentence has only just begun; you still have an eternity to go. This is absolutely grotesque. There is no possible way to overstate this point.

Due to the increasingly controversial nature of this doctrine the Evangelical Alliance commissioned a two year study on hell. The report confirmed that "there can be little doubt that the concept of hell is a biblical one. Indeed, the uncomfortable truth is that Jesus himself taught more about hell than anyone else in

---

[1] "EFC Statement of Faith," https://go.efca.org/resources/document/efca-statement-faith, (April 19, 2017).

Scripture."[2]

Hell has been consistently part of Christian theology. Second Clement, written in the early second century, declares that unbelievers are "punished with dreadful tortures in unquenchable fire" (17.7). Early fourth century church father John Chrysostom warns, "They will not be released, but will remain roasting and in such agony as cannot be expressed."[3] 18th century pull-no-punches preacher Jonathan Edwards described the plight of non-Christians: "They shall be in extreme pain, every joint of 'em, every nerve shall be full of inexpressible torment. They shall be tormented even to their fingers' ends."[4] Can you feel the love? Most modern Christians have dropped the belief in a literal fire that physically roasts people. Most aren't quite sure about the nature of the punishment, but it definitely entails sheer misery that lasts forever.

This might be shocking even to many Christians, and understandably so. For some reason pastors don't like to talk about it. Never ending punishment for nonbelievers is Christianity's best kept secret. Churchgoers will hear plenty about God's love and the forgiveness of sins. "Jesus died for you, just accept his free gift of eternal life." But you don't often hear, "or else you will spend eternity in hell." Sometimes telling the whole story can freak people out. William Crockett (writing in the 1990s) admonishes his fellow Christian leaders for not being forthright: "We hold our tongues in embarrassment, never mentioning that God will banish the wicked from his presence. Even Hollywood, with its movies like *Ghost*, has a stronger message of coming judgment than most preachers in the pulpits of America."[5]

Because church leaders are a little bashful about their

---

[2] Evangelical Alliance Commission on Unity and Truth Among Evangelicals (ACUTE), *The Nature of Hell* (London: Acute, 2000), xiiv.

[3] Ibid., 55.

[4] Quoted in William Crockett, ed., *Four Views on Hell* (Grand Rapids: Zondervan, 1996), 48.

[5] Ibid., 54.

beliefs, I'll help them out. Christians should know what they've signed up for.

Think of all the people around the world who will die today. Moms, dads, grandparents, millionaires, homeless, aid workers, maybe a serial killer, whatever, they've all inevitably fallen short of God's standards and consequently deserve to go to hell. A fraction of them (perhaps the serial killer included) will get a pass because they've come to believe that Jesus died for their sins. The rest will be in for a big surprise when they awake in horror to eternal conscious torment. It doesn't matter how nice grandma was; she's in hell and she's never leaving.

In the Evangelical Alliance's report, *The Nature of Hell*, they broach a very touchy subject. "What, for example, are we to say to terminally ill patients who have not made a commitment to Christ? Warn them of the fiery flames which await unless they convert, present the gospel's offer of new life and joy everlasting, or both?"[6] Can you imagine telling an elderly woman on her deathbed that she will soon enter everlasting torment in hell unless she converts? If you believe this is indeed her fate, can you imagine *not* warning her? Telling her she's about to go to hell might feel a bit awkward, maybe a bit tacky. But should you really worry about an awkward moment when her eternal destiny is at stake?

There's a common misconception about the Christian hell that seems to persist long after childhood. The Christian position is not that hell is for the mean people and heaven is for the nice people. No. Hitler and grandma both sinned and deserve to go to hell. But whoever confesses that Jesus is Lord will be saved, "for there is no other name under heaven that has been given among men by which we must be saved" (Acts 4.12).

Let me acknowledge up front that just because I find the Christian idea of eternal conscious torment shockingly vile, doesn't mean it's not true. I don't get to choose what's true, but such an unbelievably radical claim warrants a healthy dose of skepticism and scrutiny. Is it built on solid ground? Can

---

[6] ACUTE, 118.

Christians make sense of it? Is it believable? Keep in mind, the claim is not that an evil God will punish grandma for eternity; it's that a loving God will punish grandma for eternity. If one can square this, one can likely draw a square circle too.

JUSTICE

Defenders of hell will say things like, "Justice demands the existence of hell."[7] Let's look at the justice of the Christian system. A man abuses and rapes a girl. Fortunately he is apprehended, but the damage is done. The girl has not only endured a grievous nightmare but is also robbed of the bright future she would have had. The psychological effects of this injustice bring about further injustice. From her friendships and romantic life to her professional life, everything has been affected. Her life story is plagued by pain and struggle. It's infuriatingly unfair, but maybe justice will come in the next life. Oh wait, she's not a Christian. The rapist however undergoes a conversion in prison and accepts Jesus as his lord and savior. When he dies he enters eternal bliss. When she dies she will be punished for all eternity. Somehow that's justice in the traditional Christian worldview.

Has anybody thrown up yet? The Christian apologist would accuse me of playing on the reader's emotions by spelling out and personalizing the horrors of their doctrine. He would urge the reader not to let emotions interfere when evaluating the logic and justice of hell. "I think people should try to set aside their feelings," says J. P. Moreland, "God's decisions are not based on modern American sentimentalism. This is one of the reasons why people have never had a difficult time with the idea of hell until modern times. People today tend to care only for the softer virtues like love and tenderness, while they've forgotten the hard virtues of holiness, righteousness, and justice."[8]

---

[7] Norman L. Geisler, *Baker Encyclopedia of Christian Apologetics* (Grand Rapids: Baker, 1999), 311.

[8] J. P. Moreland in Lee Strobel, *The Case for Faith* (Grand Rapids: Zondervan, 2000), 239, 242.

Toughen up people! Don't get all sentimental about grandma. Sure, she was kind of spiritual, but she only attended church on Christmas and never confessed Jesus as her savior. She might have been a good Nana, but she wasn't perfect. She sinned against an infinite God and therefore deserves infinite punishment. This is the dispassionate logic the apologist hopes you'll buy. In their own words, it sounds like this:

- "Unredeemed sin against an infinitely good God is thus defined as infinite in consequence - that is, deserving of endless retribution."[9]
- "If the slightest sin is infinite in its significance, then it also demands infinite punishment as a divine judgement."[10]
- "Thus to sin against an infinitely glorious being is an infinitely heinous offense that is worthy of an infinitely heinous punishment."[11]

The "logic" is that sins aren't just committed against fellow human beings, they're committed against almighty God. Since grandma lost her temper occasionally, harbored some bad thoughts at times, and had premarital sex, she is not only unworthy of heaven, but deserving of being punished forever. While grandma's behavior might appear relatively innocuous to us (especially compared to that of, say, Genghis Khan), she nonetheless acted against the will of an infinite God, which means her punishment will be infinite. I guess those are the rules. Sorry grandma.

Who made up this rule, anyway? I suppose one has to make up *something* if one is going to hold that (a) God is loving and merciful, and (b) he punishes his little critters for all eternity. God's infinite righteousness demands it. There's no way around

---

[9] ACUTE, 70.

[10] John F. Walvoord in Crockett, 27.

[11] Denny Burk in Stanley N. Gundry and Preston Sprinkle, eds., Four Views on Hell (Grand Rapids: Zondervan, 2016), 20.

it. Yeah, that's it.

Challenging the majority view of his own tradition, theologian Clark Pinnock questioned, "What kind of rationale is this? What kind of God is this? Is he an unjust judge? Is it not plain that sins committed in time and space cannot deserve limitless divine retribution?"[12]

What kind of God would create such a system? Human beings, who have no say in their being born, and lack the ability to be good enough for God, will be kept alive for all eternity to suffer, unless they hear and believe the "good news." Why would God create a species that is so inherently offensive to his righteousness? This is the plan of a good, all-knowing God? Why would God create a species whose inborn behavior results in his need to respond with infinite retribution? Is anybody being honest when they say these are the actions of a merciful God?

If God needs to punish the unsaved, does it need to be forever? Isn't snuffing out non-Christians so they cease to exist forever good enough for an infinite God? Just eliminate grandma. Why keep her alive in agony with no hope? Disciplinary measures usually carry a rehabilitative purpose, but hell serves no restorative or corrective purpose. What possible reason could a good God have for *eternal* punishment?

Apparently there are a couple reasons. Moreland claims that people are too valuable for God to snuff out. "I think people in heaven will realize that hell is a way of honoring people as being intrinsically valuable creatures made in God's image . . . Hell will forever be a monument to human dignity and the value of human choice."[13] A monument to human dignity? I just threw up. Has anybody ever heard the term *motivated reasoning*?

Another reason offered for the never-ending nature of the punishment is that it "serves to demonstrate eternally the glory of God's justice."[14] Don't think of it just as God's insatiable need for vengeance. "It does have a positive aim — namely, to glorify

---

[12] Crockett, 39.

[13] Strobel, 258, 267.

[14] Denny Burk in Gundry and Sprinkle, 42.

God as a righteous Judge."[15] Norman Geisler lays it on a little thicker: "The more horrible and fearful the judgment, the brighter the sheen on the sword of God's justice . . . All people, thus are either actively or passively useful to God. In heaven believers will actively praise his mercy. In hell unbelievers will be passively useful in bringing majesty to his justice."[16] If we truly understand how pure God is and dirty grandma was, we'd understand why she must be punished forever. If this is difficult for you to see, it might be because of your post-Fall brain. As theologian Harold Brown states, "Human concepts of justice and equity, distorted as they are by the sinfulness of fallen human nature, are deceptive and unreliable."[17]

LOVE

Do I think Christianity is morally reprehensible? Well, as long as the doctrine of hell is part of it, yes, of course. It's grotesque. Do I think Christians are mean people? Of course not. I can't imagine many Christians are comfortable with hell. And I'm actually not sure how many are even clear on their church's stance on the topic. Preaching on hell is hardly en vogue. Hell is not the sell. Most churchgoers are attracted to the message of God's love, and that's what the preacher delivers. No one wants to be told that God is punishing grandma in hell. Pastors know how sick this sounds, so they avoid explicit mention of it, but find subtle ways to imply it.

Let's check in with Rick Warren again. There's no way the author of the uplifting uber-bestseller *The Purpose Driven Life* believes that non-Christians will suffer in hell forever, right?

Warren has a webpage titled "What does it mean to be saved?"[18] On it, there is a 25 minute video that explains the value

---

[15] ACUTE, 105

[16] Geisler, 314.

[17] Harold Brown, "Will the Lost Suffer Forever?" Criswell Theological Review, 4.2 (1990), 272, quoted in ACUTE, 104.

[18] Rick Warren, "What does it mean to be saved?" Online video clip, http://pastorrick.com/know-god, (accessed May 24, 2017).

of being saved and then guides viewers through a salvific prayer. Warren delivers a very warm and consoling message with words such as "No one's ever gonna love you as much as God . . . God's love is unconditional . . . No matter what you've done in life, God is not mad at you. He's mad *about* you. He loves you. . . He's a God of mercy, a God of grace, a God of compassion."

Then Warren gets down to brass tacks: "What does Jesus set us free from? All the things that mess us up: guilt, worry, resentment, bitterness, fear, loneliness." Wait. Doesn't Jesus free us from being damned to hell? I guess he doesn't believe in eternal conscious torment after all. There's no way he could forget to add something like *that* to the list. Warren continues his fairly attractive message: "I want to change — turn from hopelessness to hope, turn from darkness to light, from despair to joy, from guilt to forgiveness, from meaninglessness to purpose."

Warren does end up broaching the topic of eternity. "Eternity lies in the balance here. God wants you to live with him forever in eternity . . . Heaven's perfect and we're not. And if God let imperfect people into heaven, it wouldn't be perfect anymore . . . God has a ticket for you — for a meaningful life, a better life and an eternal life in heaven. You could never buy that ticket . . . You simply accept it . . . You believe." This is a compelling message, so why am I trying to ruin it? If he wants us to base our lives upon it, I just want to make sure we're hearing the true and full message.

In a 25 minute video explaining what it means to be saved, there is not a single mention of hell. Warren speaks of a ticket to heaven, but if one were unfamiliar with Christian theology, there would be no reason at all to suspect that the alternative to believing the "good news" is eternal punishment. Surely if he believes Jesus saves people from hell, he would talk about it when answering the question, "What does it mean to be saved." If Warren *does* believe in the eternal damnation of non-Christians, his video is similar to a nutrition label that lists some nice organic ingredients but fails to mention a few others, like cat poo and high fructose corn syrup.

When pressed by John Piper, a fellow evangelical leader, about his views on hell, Warren makes clear that he does indeed hold the party line:

Piper: Is the torment there conscious?

Warren: Oh I believe it is. And I believe it's eternal.

Piper: Yeah. Can anybody get out?

Warren: No. Of course not . . . I am motivated by the fact that in the next 365 days, 136,000 Californians will die and most of them will go into an eternity without Christ. In the next 365 days, 2.4 million American will die. Most of them will go into eternity without Christ. In the next 365 days, 74 million people in the world will go into eternity without Christ and without hope.[19]

RELAX, IT'S JUST SEPARATION

Christian leaders have developed various tactics to downplay how grotesque the doctrine of hell really is. One is to *give the impression* that hell isn't that bad — and then move on. You might hear something like this: "People have the wrong idea about hell. It's not some sort of torture chamber with hot lava and devils with pitchforks. Haha, of course not. That's ridiculous. Hell is separation from God. God lovingly allows people the freedom to carry on without him." The Christian's mind is put at ease. I guess heathens just carry on after death having keg parties, watching Cinemax, and whatever else they do without God.

The trend of summing up hell as "separation from God" is expedient for the pastor. But when examined further, this less graphic description of hell is hardly an improvement. While not holding to belief in literal fire and brimstone, the Evangelical Alliance's report does make clear that "as well as separation

---

[19] Pastorsdotcom, "John Piper Interviews Rick Warren on Hell," *YouTube*, https://youtu.be/GC6NbYQVhwA (Accessed May 24, 2017).

from God, hell involves severe punishment."[20]

In defending a metaphorical view of hell (the view that hell's endless torment does not involve actual fire), William Crockett acknowledges that the Bible's "fire" imagery has been taken literally for most of Christian history.[21] This misinterpretation, he says, inconveniently persists, rendering hell unpalatable for modern ears: "Somehow the picture of desperate faces shrieking in a lake of fire unsettles us. Trapped, we shift awkwardly on our feet and try to soften the impact of what the Bible so clearly seems to say. Christians should never be faced with this kind of embarrassment — the Bible does not support a literal view of a burning abyss."[22] Emboldened by this non-literal view, Crocket celebrates: "The doctrine of eternal punishment will never embarrass us when we preach what we know: Judgment is coming; flee the wrath of God. There is nothing here to feed the dark fantasies of twisted minds."[23] Although, he does add later that "hell would rank as the worst possible place — beyond our darkest imaginings."[24] (Apparently, there's a sweet spot between "twisted" and "our darkest imaginings.")

I'm not sure why Crockett thinks nonliteral fire will put everyone at ease. We're talking about punishing someone for all eternity. Whether there are actual flames or the flames symbolize some other kind of horror, it doesn't much matter.[25] Either way,

---

[20] ACUTE, 132.

[21] Crockett, 46.

[22] Ibid., 43-4.

[23] Ibid., 54.

[24] Ibid., 61.

[25] The entry for "Hell" in the Catholic Encyclopedia states, "Scripture and tradition speak again and again of the fire of hell, and there is no sufficient reason for taking the term as a mere metaphor." Most modern evangelicals, however, point to the Gospel of Matthew's reference to the "outer darkness" as incompatible with literal flames. Flames and darkness can't coexist, therefore the fire must be metaphorical. But maybe the fire is literal and the "outer darkness" is metaphorical, meant to convey distance from God's presence. Who cares. Either view entails unimaginable suffering that never ends.

it is the "worst possible place" and grandma can never leave. Pinnock is also left scratching his head at Crockett's logic: "Why does he leave the impression that a nonliteral view like his would make it possible to preach about hell again? It seems to me that he has painted himself into the same corner. God is a sadistic torturer."[26]

THIS IS WHAT YOU WANTED, RIGHT?

Perhaps the most common way of soft-pedaling hell is to assert that non-Christians are choosing to go there and God is simply granting their wish. A God of love cannot force people to love him. According to Moreland, "Hell is primarily a place for people who would not want to go to heaven."[27] This sounds more tolerable. Tell us more! "God is the most generous, loving, wonderful, attractive being in the cosmos. He has made us with free will and he has made us for a purpose: to relate lovingly to him and to others . . . And if we fail over and over again to live for the purpose for which we were made . . . then God will have absolutely no choice but to give us what we've asked for all along in our lives, which is separation from him."[28]

Does anybody actually ask to go to hell? Is God really just granting people's wishes to be kept alive in never ending anguish? Of course not. This is all spin. Moreland is classifying non-Christians as "people who would not want to go to heaven." God will give non-Christians what they've "asked for all along." What else could the infidel possibly expect? "To think that a person could go through their whole life constantly ignoring him, constantly mocking him by the way they choose to live without him, saying, 'I couldn't care less about what you put me here to do. I couldn't care less about your values or your Son's death for me.'"[29]

---

[26] Crockett, 88.

[27] Strobel, 247.

[28] Ibid., 241.

[29] Ibid., 252.

With the this-is-what-you-always-wanted argument, the apologist is banking on some sleight of hand. Not being a Christian is tantamount to thumbing one's nose at God. Apparently, non-Christians know Christianity is true but choose to ignore and mock God. It doesn't seem to occur to the apologist that maybe some people just don't think Christianity is true. Is the Christian worldview so obviously true that anyone who doesn't hold it must be engaged in active rebellion? It's definitely not obviously true to me (if you haven't noticed). If someone thought their beliefs would land them in hell, they would change their beliefs accordingly. To say that non-Christians want to go to hell instead of heaven is disingenuous at best.

And then there's the glaring problem of followers of other religions. Is the Sikh, the Muslim, or the Mormon really trying to ignore or mock God? Obviously not. As far as they know, they are seeking and following God as they are meant to do. Apologist William Lane Craig equates the non-Christian with "the drowning man who consistently pushes the life preserver away that has been thrown to him."[30] This might ease the Christian's mind, but it's not what's happening in real life.

Saying "Hell is primarily a place for people who would not want to go to heaven" is silliness. The apologist is left with this: People who are not Christians are, *in effect*, "choosing" to go to hell. Which is the same as saying "non-Christians go to hell." Which is just restating the very claim that the argument was meant to sugarcoat. The this-is-what-you-always-wanted argument is a desperate attempt to repackage an unpalatable belief.

THE DOCTRINE FROM HELL

I'd like to respectfully put Christians to the test. On one hand I have sympathy for Christians who are stuck with the task

---

[30] William Lane Craig, "Doctrine of Christ (part 28)," *Defenders* Series 2, Podcast Transcript, May 20, 2012, http://www.reasonablefaith.org/defenders-2-podcast/transcript/s6-28#ixzz4N5eWy5y5.

of defending such an awful belief. It must be confusing. But on the other hand, because this belief is so awful, it needs to be confronted head on. I'll offer up a scenario to see if Christianity really makes sense to you.

Let's say you have been sharing your faith with two teenagers whose parents recently died in an accident. Their parents were responsible, loving parents, who had a vague belief in a higher power, but never came to a saving relationship with the Lord. What is the "good news" that you share with the orphaned teenagers? Will you inform them that we are all sinners who deserve eternal punishment, but they have a chance to be saved?

When they connect the dots and say something like "Wait a second, are you telling me my parents are in hell!" what will you say? Will you lie? Will you make something up, like "heaven is for nice people and hell is for criminals"? That's not the gospel. Will you say, "They're probably in hell, but we don't know for sure"?

Let's say you decide to boldly own the doctrine of hell (as you should if you believe it). You've read some apologetics (the discipline of defending the faith) and maybe now is a good time to try out the arguments: "I know it's hard to accept that your parent's punishment will never end, but the severity of God's punishment demonstrates how righteous he truly is." Or maybe, "God is simply honoring your parent's free will. This is what they always wanted – to live without God." Or, if you're really feeling ambitious, "If you could set aside your emotions, I think you could see that this is what your parents deserve." Obviously this is all sickeningly disgusting. The point is that there might be something terribly wrong with your faith if sharing it makes you feel filthy all over.

DANCING AROUND

Denny Burk, Bible teacher from Boyce College, summarizes the traditional Christian view on hell: "All those who fail to experience saving faith in Jesus while they are alive in this age will be resurrected and condemned when Christ returns. They will then be cast into hell where they will suffer never-ending punishment."[31] Most Christians try not to advertise this position, so it lives quietly in the background. Being "saved" (to use Protestant language) is at the heart of the gospel, but many Christian leaders have become adept at not being too explicit about *what* one is saved from. One way to do this is to focus on the fate of the believer, not the unbeliever. The believer gains "eternal life" or will "enter the kingdom." When speaking of the unbelievers, who will suffer eternity in hell, they can be referred to as simply "lost" or "dead in their sins" – fairly innocuous terms that don't evoke images of being kept alive in agony for eternity.

Despite the dearth of direct references to hell, the doctrine is still in operation. It's in the traditional confessions of faith and either assumed or explicit in modern "what we believe" statements of Christian schools and churches. Some are braver than others, declaring plainly that one can only be saved through faith in Jesus (an unpopular message in a diverse world). William Lane Craig, for example, states, "We believe that salvation from sin and eternal life are available only through Jesus Christ's atoning death on the cross . . . There is no salvation outside of Christ."[32] But from my experiences, leaders and laymen alike go especially limp on their belief in hell when confronted directly about real, specific people going there.

When presenting believers with specific non-Christians, such as grandma or Gandhi, one might hear something like, "It's not my job to decide who gets into heaven. I leave that up to God." So, is it a total mystery? Is it a surprise? Maybe you don't know *for sure* who gets into heaven and who is damned to hell, but what does your religion suggest about grandma's and Gandhi's current state of wellbeing? Biola, one of the foremost Christian universities, declares in their doctrinal statement that those who do not receive Jesus Christ as their Savior and Lord in

---

[31] Gundry and Sprinkle, 20.

[32] Craig, "Doctrine of Christ (part 28)," *Defenders* Series 2.

this present life "shall be raised from the dead and throughout eternity exist in the state of conscious, unutterable, endless torment of anguish."[33] This sounds quite clear to me. I know one can't be *absolutely* sure about specific people, but clearly Christianity is not silent on the issue of salvation. If one believes Christianity is true, one can't think grandma and Gandhi are having much fun right now. Many likely reject what their religion says, and assume a more intuitive position: "Hell isn't for grandmas, parents, and people we know; it's for bad people like Osama Bin Laden and Bill Nye." Maybe this *is* what most Christians believe. If so, it helps prove my point that Christianity no longer makes sense.

The next tactic to avoid the conclusion that God is infinitely punishing a specific person might be something like, "Maybe Gandhi secretly converted to Christianity. I don't know his heart when he died." Ok, maybe he did (maybe Stalin did too), but this is a total red herring (trying to avoid the reality of what Christianity teaches by offering up an unlikely what-if). Maybe grandma quietly converted to Islam on her deathbed. Who knows. It's unlikely that grandma swapped out worldviews just before she died, but let's grant that it's logically possible that she converted to Christianity in her final moments. Does it really get Christianity off the hook to say there's a small chance she's not in hell? No. The Christian is actually just admitting that unless this unlikely event happened, grandma is indeed experiencing horrendous eternal torment. In other words, grandma is *almost certainly* in hell . . . but we can't be absolutely positive.

A third way to avoid facing the hideousness of hell is to simply say, "I trust God to do what's right." In other words, "I'm not really gonna think about it." Ok, well your religion says that God will punish the majority of humanity for eternity, maybe you should think about it. Maybe this is a red flag. If you're comfortable with circular reasoning (my religion says nonbelievers go to hell, therefore punishing nonbelievers in hell

---

33 Biola University Doctrinal Statement, https://www.biola.edu/about/doctrinal-statement, (May 24, 2017).

must be moral), please don't criticize the morality or logic of other religions. You have no legs to stand on. If you can accept eternal conscious punishment, you can accept anything.

WHAT A MESS

As if the task of rationalizing the morality of a creator who eternally punishes his creatures for falling short of his impossible standards isn't difficult enough, the Christian also has to contend with the logistics of such a system. Anatomically modern humans have existed for about 200,000 years. This idea that we need a savior to die for our sins as a means to avoid eternal punishment popped up a mere 2,000 years ago in a small corner of the globe. There were loads of other thriving societies who had independently developed their own gods, rituals, and stories of creation and afterlife. In most cases, these societies knew nothing of each other. The ancient Chinese, American Indians, and Aboriginal Australians were completely unaware that some far-off religion had them slated for hell (of course they could be saved by Jesus . . . if they knew about him). In fact, even the Jews, whose scriptures constitute the Christian Old Testament, didn't know about this unfortunate predicament humanity was in. They were never awaiting a savior who could finally open up a path for them to avoid eternal damnation. Christian theology was sloppily grafted onto the Hebrew scriptures. If the Christian hell were true, it would be quite a secret to keep under wraps for thousands of years. Surprise!

And this is one of the most bizarre and overlooked aspects of Christianity. In order for the "good news" to make any sense, the messenger must first inform non-Christians that there is very bad news — that they're going to be punished for eternity when they die. Evangelist Ajith Fernando worries Christians might forget to share this part: "If our hearers don't realize that there is judgment to come, they may not see the need to be saved and thus not realize the goodness of the good news."[34] Is the irony not obvious? The "good news" is predicated on the news that the large majority of people who ever existed will suffer endlessly in hell. As Norman Geisler puts it, we "are born on a road that leads to hell."[35]

If one believes the Christian system of salvation is true, one must wonder about the fate of all those humans who never heard the story of Jesus. The majority of human history happened before Jesus was born. "The unevangelized," as they're often called, never even had the chance to be saved from eternal conscious torment. Even after Jesus' crucifixion, it took 1,500 years for the Europeans to bring disease, enslavement, and the good news of salvation to the vast civilizations of the Americas. Did all the pre-Columbian Native Americans go to hell? Shortly after the Europeans arrived, the African slave trade was shifted into high gear. Were the Africans who were seized from their homes to be enslaved in the Americas the lucky ones? They could now be Christianized, and their souls saved. But what about the fate of the millions of slaves who died in transport before reaching the message of salvation in the New World?

Maybe God has a different measuring stick for these millions of souls who lived outside the scope of Christ. Automatic eternal punishment for everyone who has never heard of Jesus strikes some Christians as unfair, maybe even demented. Perhaps God judges the unevangelized by their actions? Maybe God has a scale that weighs good deeds against bad deeds. Whichever way the scale tips indicates the eternal fate of that person. But this option is precluded by the belief that any sin at all cannot be tolerated by a righteous and just God. Furthermore, if there was *already* a path open to heaven, then Jesus didn't need to die. Christians are in a pickle. The orthodox theologian is loath to mess with the belief that Jesus' atoning

---

[34] Ajith Fernando, Crucial Questions About Hell (Wheaton, IL: Crossway Books, 1991), 180.

[35] Geisler, 315.

death on the cross is the only way to salvation. The great Christian commission is to go out and save "the lost." What's the urgency in reaching these distant heathens if God has already provided them with another track to salvation? And if they're already getting into heaven, what is this "good news" that the evangelist brings?

William Lane Craig, Christian philosopher and apologist, tries to thread this needle. He suggests that the unevangelized (those who have never heard of Jesus) do have access to salvation, but "hardly anybody, if anybody," is actually saved.[36] It's technically *possible* to get saved without knowing about Jesus, but virtually never happens, so the urgent need to share the gospel is unaffected. In the Bible, Romans 1 and 2 indicate that whether one has heard of Jesus or not, all are without excuse. God has revealed himself through *natural revelation* (i.e. through nature and in our consciences). Even though one might have never heard of the biblical God or the story of Jesus, one must still properly respond to natural revelation by acknowledging one's moral failings and throwing one's self at the feet of the one true God for forgiveness. But that's not what the heathens do; they go on in their sin, worshipping their little fake gods. So, the rationale goes, even without specific knowledge of the Jesus story, the unevangelized are justly condemned. (Most theologians are clear that even *if* any of the unevangelized are saved, the sacrificial death of Jesus was still necessary — so technically there still is only *one* way.)

While Craig believes the unevangelized get what they deserve, he is still troubled by the unequal opportunity for salvation. What if some of the Native Americans who were condemned by natural revelation, *would have* been saved if they had only been presented with the clearer, more powerful revelation of Jesus Christ? Doesn't God want everybody to be saved? Why would God damn people to hell who *would have* embraced the gospel if only they'd heard it? Craig proposes a

---

[36] Craig, "Doctrine of Christ (part 28)," *Defenders* Series 2.

solution:

> There are no such people. God in his providence has so
> arranged the world that those who would respond to the
> gospel if they heard it, do hear it. Those who do not respond to
> God's general revelation in nature and conscience and never
> hear the gospel wouldn't have responded to the gospel even if
> they had heard it. And thus no one is lost because of historical
> and geographical accidents. Indeed there are no accidents on
> this view of history and geography. Anyone who wants to be
> saved or even *would* want to be saved will be saved. Now how
> can God get any better than that?[37]

According to Craig's proposal, all the pre-Jesus people
(except maybe a few) are in hell because they *would have* rejected
Christianity no matter where or when they were born. Craig
doesn't care how believable this scenario is. As long as it's
logically possible, he feels he's out of a tight spot. These are the
sorts of surmisings Christians must concoct to support their
system of salvation.

Even in a world widely familiar with Christianity, logistical
problems abound. Think about all the people around the world
who seek God and a spiritual life, but are not Christians.
People's beliefs are influenced by their surroundings. This is
quite clear when mapping religious beliefs on the globe. Does
the Christian wonder why God's salvific work is so
geographically disproportionate? Why are the chances of going
to hell so much higher for those born in Japan or Iran than for
those in the United States? Would God really make one's
country of origin a leading factor in determining eternal destiny?
How about the influence parents have on their children's beliefs?
Is someone going to suggest that God providentially arranges
for those who *would* believe in the right context to be born of
Christian parents?

---

[37] William Lane Craig, "Doctrine of Christ (part 30)," *Defenders* Series 2, Podcast
transcript, June 24, 2012, http://www.reasonablefaith.org/defenders-2-
podcast/transcript/s6-30.

Becoming a Christian depends on believing a certain story. Let's say an intelligent, socially-gifted evangelist shares the gospel with Jack, but a second-rate evangelist shares the gospel with Jill. Jack is convinced and goes to heaven. Jill is unmoved and ends up in hell. What about a Hindu with a mental disability, such as Down syndrome? Is he held accountable for not holding the correct beliefs? What about someone who doesn't have a genetic disorder, but is just not very bright? Will she be condemned for not settling on the correct worldview? The uncontrollable factors that lead to one's beliefs are numerous and obvious. Does this sound like a well thought out, sensible, and loving system for determining who will be punished forever? Or one that resulted from a haphazard process that faithful theologians are now duty-bound to rationalize?

And what of the eternal fate of infants and children who pass away? The fact that this question even needs to be asked is frightening, but it's a question that Christian theologians have wrestled with throughout Christian history. In the Catholic tradition, infant baptism serves to wash away the guilt from Adam's sin. "[Adam] has transmitted to us a sin with which we are all born afflicted, a sin which is the 'death of the soul.' Because of this certainty of faith, the Church baptizes for the remission of sins even tiny infants who have not committed personal sin."[38] Even without living long enough to commit one's own sins, *original sin* ensures that all are born guilty and in peril.

In the *Baker Encyclopedia of Christian Apologetics*, Norman Geisler lays out the historical positions on infant salvation.[39] Augustine (early 5th century), concluded that unbaptized babies are indeed condemned because of their inherited depravity. Other major Western thinkers, such as Ambrose and Aquinas, were clear that unbaptized babies were barred from heaven, but as they dwelt in hell, they would at least be spared of the pain. This sentiment gave rise to a third option, limbo, for some in the

---

[38] Catechism, 403.

[39] Geisler, 360-6.

Catholic tradition. Unbaptized infants who died would experience limbo, a neutral place between heaven and hell.

For the Protestant theologian, personal faith, not sacraments, such as baptism, is what is required for salvation. How can a baby, born in Adam's sin, who hasn't displayed faith in Christ, be admitted to heaven? Geisler sets forth some alternatives. The Westminster Confession of Faith states, "*Elect infants, dying in infancy, are regenerated, and saved by Christ*" (10.3). In this Calvinist theology, the "elect" are the ones whom God chose to save. The unelect babies, whom God did not choose, go to hell. Another possibility is that God will base his judgment on what the infant *would have* believed. Geisler states, "God, as an omniscient Being, foreknew which infants would have believed if they had lived long enough."[40]

Perhaps due to how obscene this topic is, the most popular view today is that all children who die before a certain age will be saved. A so-called *age of accountability* is proposed. If a child dies before this age, often speculated to be around twelve years old, the child is automatically admitted into heaven. But after crossing this threshold, the child must have made the proper faith commitment to avoid damnation. It's nice that most Christians probably don't believe God will punish kids under twelve for eternity in hell, but this workaround is still unsettling. This belief entails some precise instant in a child's life, before which, if he dies he will enter eternal bliss. But if he dies one second after this instant, God will punish him forever, unless of course he holds the "correct" beliefs at this moment. Again, look at the kind of scaffolding one must construct to support the uncomfortable implications of Christian salvation. The point is not that an age of accountability is logically impossible (an omnipotent being can make up whatever rules it wants). But is this really a system that a rational, loving God would put in place? Is this the God Christians believe in?

In 2011 Rob Bell, a popular Christian author and former pastor of a large congregation, had the courage to question the

---

[40] Ibid., 362.

doctrine of hell in a book titled *Love Wins*. Even though church leaders don't tend to celebrate their belief in hell, Bell's challenging of it set off alarm bells in the evangelical world. One of their own, questioning the classical understanding of salvation! Bell writes, "If every new baby being born could grow up to *not* believe the right things and go to hell forever, then prematurely terminating a child's life anytime from conception to twelve years of age would actually be the loving thing to do, guaranteeing that the child ends up in heaven, and not hell, forever. Why run the risk?"[41] I can't find fault with his logic. If the consequence for not being a Christian is being punished forever, dying young when salvation is guaranteed, is a small price to pay. Holding to an age-of-accountability also implies that aborted (and miscarried) embryos and fetuses are extremely fortunate. They get an eternity of bliss, with no risk of ever facing God's eternal wrath. I'm not sure how many Christians factor this into their views on abortion.

One can always play the *mystery* card. A follower of any religion can leapfrog any difficulty by appealing to "God's mysterious ways." But at some point, when the red flags keep piling up, one should wonder if perhaps one is on the wrong track. Maybe it's not a mystery. Maybe it's just wrong.

IS HELL FREEZING OVER?

I have to think that the majority of Christians deep down don't *actually* believe this stuff. Granted many Christians only hear an occasional whitewashed version of hell and don't spend much time working through their theology. But even for those who claim to hold the belief, they don't seem to behave as if it's true. If Christians genuinely think their family, friends, and even strangers are headed for such a fate, they should be pleading with them, ceaselessly finding ways to convince the unbeliever. Preacher and author John Blanchard tries to rouse his fellow Christians: "How can you possibly accept that multitudes of

---

[41] Rob Bell, *Love Wins* (New York: HarperOne, 2011), 4.

people — including many you know personally — are on a collision course with an announcement of God's righteous and terrifying condemnation and yet do nothing to warn them of their danger?"[42] I suspect the answer is that most Christians don't genuinely believe it. Family and friends enduring "terrifying condemnation" for eternity is much too ghastly and bewildering to actually be true. And it's grotesquely at odds with most modern Christians' conceptions of God.

The modern world in which the Christian lives is an uneasy fit for the God of the Bible. Once upon a time, fear of hell permeated Christian societies. In fact, torture was readily employed to save the misguided heretic. I think we're all thankful that most of us now live in a culture where heresy and unbelief go unpunished. But the secularization of Western culture has made Christianity less relatable. Natural selection has thereupon acted to give the Christian God a makeover. Today, he is generally softer and not nearly as fearsome. In case we forget, this is the God who hardened Pharaoh's heart in order to continue inflicting punishment on Pharaoh's people. With a supernaturally hardened heart, Pharaoh was helpless to avoid God's final curse: the killing of every firstborn in Egypt, "from the firstborn of the Pharaoh who sits on his throne, even to the firstborn of the slave girl who is behind the millstones; all the firstborn of the cattle as well" (Exod. 11.5). This not-so-fuzzy God of yore conformed much more easily to the belief in fiery damnation for nonbelievers. These biblical stories are of course still found in the Bible, but apologists soften them for modern ears and then modern brains somehow chalk them up to how God used to be, in some distant reality.

God has been rebranded. No longer do preachers preach of the torments of hell. Though just a few centuries ago, the popular Jonathan Edwards spoke unequivocally of the dangers facing the unsaved:

To unconverted Persons in this Congregation. This that you have

---

[42] ACUTE, 113.

heard is the Case of every one of you that are out of Christ. That World of Misery, that Lake of burning Brimstone is extended abroad under you. There is the dreadful Pit of the glowing Flames of the Wrath of God; there is Hell's wide gaping Mouth open; and you have nothing to stand upon, not any Thing to take hold of: there is nothing between you and Hell but the Air.[43]

With the plethora of churches today offering slick presentations from hip, motivational pastors, I'm not sure an Edwards-like message is well-suited for the free market forces of today's church landscape. Just for fun, let's picture Edwards preaching in one of our modern megachurches. Behold the transition from his frightful message of God's torturous wrath to the emo-drenched, metrosexual sounds of the modern church band. Anyway . . .

Some within Christianity, such as Christian apologist Greg Koukl, are disheartened by the growing lack of conviction: "There are a lot of people on the inside who are starting to bend, they're giving in, and they're letting go of something foundational and essential, that is the existence of the place where God does eternal justice: Hell."[44] In reviewing Rob Bell's book *Love Wins* (in which he suggests the possibility that *all* might be saved), Mark Galli, editor of *Christianity Today* warns, "To demythologize one doctrine is to make the others less coherent."[45] Galli voices a common concern: Bell is operating on a slippery slope — a slope that can slide into the amorphous theology of liberal Christianity.

The call to go out into the world and save souls has driven Christian missionaries to the far reaches of the earth. William Lane Craig laments, "I find it ironic that we here in the 21st century, who are on the verge of completing the task of world

---

[43] Jonathan Edwards, "Sinners in the Hands of an Angry God," preached July 8, 1741.

[44] Greg Koukl, "Hell and the Gospel," May 9, 2013, https://www.str.org/articles/hell-and-the-gospel#.WSXsCevyuUk, (May 24, 2017).

[45] Mark Galli, "Rob Bell's Bridge Too Far," *Christianity Today*, March 14, 2011, http://www.christianitytoday.com/ct/2011/april/lovewins.html (May 24, 2017).

evangelization — we have the manpower, we have the money, we have the technology to complete the task of the Great Commission in our lifetimes — I find it so ironic that as we are on the threshold of doing so, it should be the church's own theologians who should try to trip her at the finish line."[46]

Even the Catholic Church, which is encumbered by a two thousand year paper trail of official beliefs, is showing movement. The Fourth Lateran Council in the year 1215 produced very clear statements, such as "There is one Universal Church of the faithful, outside of which there is absolutely no salvation" (Canon 1). Fast forward to the 1960s. The Second Vatican Council issued a document which cites Hinduism and Buddhism, acknowledging that there is good in other religions.[47] The document then praises Muslims and Jews. It never declares that salvation can be found through these other religions, but the conciliatory message leaves one wondering how God could then damn these people to hell. Even more recently the Catholic Church issued a report titled, "The Hope of Salvation for Infants who Die Without Being Baptised."[48] The report concludes that there is "hope that infants who die without baptism may be saved and brought into eternal happiness," but we don't know for sure.

To the credit of Catholics, they have evolved — more than they can get away with admitting. The Catholic Church has opened up to modern scholarship (both biblical and scientific), though due to their structure and age, are still tethered to traditional positions. Having taken some classes at Catholic seminaries, I would venture to say there is a significant gulf between the personal views of much of the clergy (and even the

---

[46] William Lane Craig, "Doctrine of Christ (part 26)," *Defenders* Series 2, Podcast Transcript, May 6, 2012, http://www.reasonablefaith.org/defenders-2-podcast/transcript/s6-26.

[47] Pope Paul VI, *Nostra aetate*, October 28, 1965, http://www.vatican.va/archive/hist_councils/ii_vatican_council/documents/vat-ii_decl_19651028_nostra-aetate_en.html, (May 24, 2017).

[48] International Theological Commission, "The Hope of Salvation for Infants who Die Without Being Baptised."

Pope!) and official Catholic doctrine. Do they still believe eternal hellfire awaits all those outside the church? I would guess most Catholics do not.

TRADITIONALISM VS. CONDITIONALISM

Eternal conscious torment is increasingly evaded. Is Christianity stuck with it? What is a Christian to do? One option is to embrace a liberal interpretation of Christianity. One might conclude that beliefs such as the Fall, the atonement, and eternal conscious torment are antiquated ideas that don't need to be preserved (see Appendix). Perhaps the core of Christianity is following Jesus' moral teachings: the golden rule, charity for the poor and disadvantaged, etc. But for others, abandoning core tenets of the faith, such as salvation through Jesus' atoning death on the cross, is a bridge too far. A second option is gaining popularity. The back cover of the book *The Nature of Hell* reads, "Evangelicals have traditionally held that unbelievers will be condemned without exception to eternal conscious punishment. However, increasing numbers of evangelical thinkers are declaring sympathy for *conditional immortality*."[49]

Conditional immortality is the belief that immortality, living forever, is conditioned upon accepting Jesus. It is often referred to as *conditionalism* or *annihilationism* (those who do not come to a saving relationship with Jesus will be annihilated, not kept alive in torment forever). The view can accommodate differing degrees of punishment prior or during annihilation (perhaps Genghis Khan is annihilated in a more torturous fashion than grandma is, for example).

Whether annihilation or eternal conscious punishment is more biblical, I do not know. My view is that the Bible does not speak with one coherent voice on the matter of life after death. The Bible is a compilation of writings from different people from different times and places. As an article of faith, one can choose

---

[49] ACUTE, back cover.

to believe that the Bible speaks with a unified voice. I can see how believing this is desirable and even necessary at some level, but I'm not sure what else would lead someone to this conclusion. Regardless, what is clear is that eternal punishment is the traditional view, and annihilationism/conditionalism is a minority view that is currently gaining traction.

For conditionalists, humans are mortal by default, but Jesus offers a way to live forever. Conditionalism is enormously less repugnant than eternal conscious punishment. Instead of keeping grandma alive forever so she can serve out her endless sentence in abject misery, she dies. Even if the annihilationist posits that God will torture her for a while before she's finally extinguished, this pales in comparison to everlasting punishment. In fact, this is such a different picture of God, that I would say conditionalists and traditionalists are effectively worshipping different Gods.

Clark Pinnock, an influential advocate of conditional immortality, backs me up on this: "Everlasting torment is intolerable from a moral point of view because it makes God into a bloodthirsty monster who maintains an everlasting Auschwitz for victims whom he does not even allow to die. How is one to worship or imitate such a cruel and merciless God?"[50] This is a point of distinction that matters.

Committed conditionalists can avoid some of the objections to hell, but Christians in general don't get to bypass these objections by straddling the fence: "Well *maybe* God doesn't punish people for eternity. Crisis averted." No. Consider the statement, "My neighbor may or may not torture puppies." A whole lot hinges upon which is true. This isn't some throwaway variable that can be left out of the equation. He's an entirely different person if it turns out he's a serial puppy torturer. I hope your perception of this person would be highly dependent on this fact.

If conditional immortality is true, Christians have had the

---

[50] Clark Pinnock, "The Destruction of the Finally Impenitent," *A Journal from the Radical Reformation*, Fall 1992, Vol. 2, No. 1., p. 15.

wrong idea about God through church history — and this raises another issue. As Crockett argues, "When someone proposes to change a doctrine taught consistently since the inception of the church, it should make us wonder how everyone throughout the centuries could have been so terribly wrong."[51] Yes, and this would be a terribly large point to be wrong about.

When interpreting what the Bible says about hell, the Evangelical Alliance urges fellow Christians to "look to the Holy Spirit to illuminate us and lead us into the truth." But that doesn't appear to work. Once again, the Holy Spirit seems to be telling Christians different things. Will the real Holy Spirit please stand up? Is the Spirit responsible for the growing popularity of conditional immortality? Why has eternal conscious torment been the consistent majority view through the ages? Has the Holy Spirit been asleep at the wheel? Did the Holy Spirit view the teaching that God would punish unbelievers for all eternity as a trivial misunderstanding that wasn't worth nitpicking?

While a God who does not punish his little creatures for eternity is much more palatable than one who does, the conditionalist is still not relieved of the messiness and illogic of the Christian system of salvation discussed earlier. Salvation is still dependent on hearing a particular story and believing it is true. Modern humans show up around 200,000 years ago, but God waits 198,000 years to unveil the true religion, which offers a way to avoid annihilation? Meanwhile vast stretches of earth remain completely isolated from the salvific message for hundreds of years. Do non-Christian children get annihilated? Why are the odds of being annihilated so much higher in Asia than in America? Are cultural differences leading to high levels of Chinese and Japanese annihilation? Are Asians genetically more prone to hate God? Is God not trying as hard in that part of the world?

When one tries to map this system onto reality it strains credibility. It is of course *possible* that no matter how far-fetched they seem, the Christian doctrines of damnation and salvation

---

[51] Crockett, 62-63.

are true. It's *possible* any number of unfalsifiable claims are true, but when problems litter the landscape, one should be very skeptical. And let's not forget these beliefs are built around an event that never happened: the Fall. Oh, and is the Bible the kind of book that should give us the confidence to believe in hell? Turn the page to find out.

6. THE GOD OF THE BIBLE

Christians turn to the Bible to gain otherwise unknowable truths about creation, salvation, and even the future. Underlying these efforts is the assumption that the Bible is a supernatural book, one that humans alone could have never created. God worked through the human authors, editors, and later compilers to deliver us this exact book.[1] But why make this assumption? Why, for example, should we believe that the author of the Book of Revelation knew anything at all about what happens to people after they die? Why think the ancient authors of Genesis knew how the world began, or that there was a couple named Adam and Eve that screwed up the human race? I have no doubt that a God powerful enough to create the universe, could produce an astonishing book. But is the Bible such a book?

The Bible is fascinating. It's a window into our past. We see our predecessors' wrestling with the challenges and mysteries of existence. In these ancient words we can find wisdom that potentially enhances our lives.

When we come across the Golden Rule, "Treat people the same way you want them to treat you" (Matt. 7.12), we think, "Yeah, that's a good one. Thanks Jesus, great advice!" We don't

---

[1] Although Protestants, Catholics, and Eastern Orthodox disagree about which books should be included in the Bible.

want to live in a society where we are readily lied to, robbed, enslaved, or killed. We see how this basic teaching of respecting others promotes a community in which we and our children can flourish. We don't decide the Golden Rule is a good idea because it's in the Bible; we like it because it makes sense. It should be no surprise that it has independently cropped up in disparate societies through history.

But the Bible, especially the Old Testament, also says some strange and disturbing things: "If men get into a fight with one another, and the wife of one intervenes to rescue her husband from the grip of his opponent by reaching out and seizing his genitals, you shall cut off her hand; show no pity" (Deut. 25.11-12). When we read this, we think, "Ummm. For some reason this verse isn't resonating with me as much as that golden-rule one." And for good reason. The hand-chopping rule is irrational and cruel. The woman's husband is getting beat up. If she's desperate to save him, targeting the other man's genitals might be an understandable move. Cutting off the woman's hand for such an action sounds like something ISIS might do. "Show no pity," the Bible adds. Is this the kind of book the creator of the universe writes?

Christians have of course come up with "explanations" for the myriad of problematic verses. Paul Copan, who authored a book intended to defend the morality of the God of the Bible, suggests that the words "you shall cut off her hand," are probably mistranslated.[2] That's good to hear. A better translation, he argues, is "you shall shave her groin." Wait, what? First off, I can't find a Bible that uses this wording. It's hard to believe Copan's is the better translation when all the Bible translation committees disagree with him. Second, this new punishment of shaving her pubic hair is also barbaric. Copan tries to rationalize it as "public humiliation for publicly humiliating the man,"[3] which is far more humane than mutilation (cutting off her hand). Maybe, but it's still

---

[2] Paul Copan, *Is God a Moral Monster?* (Grand Rapids: Baker Books, 2011), 121.
[3] Ibid., 122.

disturbingly perverse. The question we need to continually come back to is *What makes more sense, that these are the words of the creator of the universe or the words of ancient people?*

DEFENDING BARBARITY

The point of this chapter is not to attack the Bible, but to attack the idea that the Bible is the perfect word of God, divinely inspired, or even authoritative in any meaningful way. I'm definitely not the first to point out what sure looks like atrocious behavior from the biblical God. This is a glaring problem for Christianity. And, naturally, Christian apologists have fought back. Their proposed explanations can provide helpful context, an alternate translation, or a more charitable interpretation of a troubling passage. Some efforts are more believable than others, but ultimately it's too heavy a lift. The barbarity the apologists attempt to excuse is at times so flagrant one wonders what the God of the Bible would have to say or do to lose their support. But I suppose if believers are unalterably committed to the position that the Bible is the infallible word of God, they have no choice but to rationalize whatever the good book throws at them.

There's a general principle Christian apologists often invoke that is worth discussing up front. To account for God's allegedly immoral commands and behavior, they argue, we must first acknowledge the preexisting culture in which God was forced to operate. Patriarchy, slavery, polygamy, and savage war practices were all part of ancient Near Eastern life. Copan refers to these practices as "fallen social arrangements"[4] (You remember the Fall, right?). God was working within fallen, flawed and ingrained systems. Completely overhauling Israelite social structures was not a realistic option. Copan explains, "[God] meets his people where they are while seeking to show them a higher ideal in the context of ancient Near Eastern life. . . . God didn't impose legislation that Israel wasn't ready for." The

---

[4] Ibid., 60-62.

claim is that God's law was temporary and less than ideal, but better than that of Israel's neighbors. A pretty low bar they set for God, if you ask me.

First, this does admit that God condoned immoral behavior (just not as immoral as the behavior of Israel's neighbors). Second, one must now wonder which Bible verses were mere accommodations to a morally inferior culture and which are actually real. But most importantly, was this really the best a perfect being could do? As we survey specific examples of the biblical God's words and actions, ask yourself if the "accommodation" defense really makes sense.

ANIMAL SACRIFICE

The God of Israel in the Old Testament is named *Yahweh*. Most Bible translations follow the convention of replacing the name YHWH (i.e. Yahweh when vowels are inserted) with "the LORD." So when you read "the LORD" (all caps, smaller font) in your Bible, the underlying Hebrew is YHWH, the personal name of the biblical God. (From here on, "the LORD" will read "Yahweh" in all relevant Bible verses.)

Yahweh behaved a lot like other gods of the ancient Near East. For example, gods used to demand and enjoy animal sacrifices. Yahweh was no different. Specific instructions on proper sacrifice pervade the Bible: "He shall slay the young bull before Yahweh; and Aaron's sons the priests shall offer up the blood and sprinkle the blood around on the altar . . . And the priest shall offer up in smoke all of it on the altar for a burnt offering, an offering by fire of a soothing aroma to Yahweh" (Lev. 1.5-9).

As Old Testament scholar Michael Coogan explains, sacrifice could have several functions "including appeasing an angry deity, thanking a supportive deity, or motivating a deity to help the offerer."[5] He adds, "The deity was pleased by the

---

[5] Michael D. Coogan, *The Old Testament: A Historical and Literary Introduction to the Hebrew Scriptures* (New York: Oxford, 2006), 139.

odor of the sacrifice." This is indeed what we find in the Bible: "Then Noah built an altar to Yahweh, and took of every clean animal and of every clean bird and offered burnt offerings on the altar. **Yahweh smelled the soothing aroma**; and Yahweh said to Himself, 'I will never again curse the ground on account of man'" (Gen. 8.20-21).

Like other gods, Yahweh was particular about which animals he would accept. He told Moses "it must be perfect to be accepted; there shall be no defect in it" (Lev. 22.21-24). Yahweh rejected animals that were blind or maimed, had a limb that was too long or short, and even animals with crushed testicles. He also showed a preference for male animals.

Similarly, the physical appearance of priests mattered to Yahweh. He told Moses that no one with a defect was allowed to give him his food at the altar (Lev. 21.16). Yahweh listed some of the people he wanted to keep at a distance: "a blind man, or a lame man, or he who has a disfigured face, or any deformed limb, or a man who has a broken foot or broken hand, or a hunchback or a dwarf, or one who has a defect in his eye or eczema or scabs or crushed testicles" (Lev 21.18-20). The reason Yahweh didn't want these people around was simply "because he has a defect" and "so that he will not profane My sanctuaries" (Lev. 21.23).

Bringing Yahweh's attitude towards people with physical differences into the churches that worship him today would be incredibly offensive. Imagine churches today not allowing dwarfs in the sanctuary. Dwarfs can still listen to the sermon, but from a special outer room so as not to profane the sacred space. This might sound strange to us today, but this sentiment was normal for gods back then. Assyriologist A. H. Sayce said of the priest in the Babylonian tradition, "It was necessary that he should be without bodily blemish. The leper, the blind, and the maimed were excluded from the service of the gods."[6] Was Yahweh just trying to fit in with other gods?

---

[6] A. H. Sayce, *The Religions of Ancient Egypt and Babylonia* (Edinburgh: T. & T. Clark, 1902), 465.

Sacrifices were a way to keep favor with the gods. Happy gods, happy life, as they say. Yahweh made a covenant with the Israelites. He would take care of his chosen people and they would worship him exclusively. Yahweh provided the Israelites with laws for proper worship and proper living. If the Israelites obeyed, life would be good, if not, things could get very ugly.

Peace, prosperity, calamity and suffering all flow from God. This is the predominant view in the Bible. "I form the light, and create darkness: I make peace, and create evil: I Yahweh do all these things" (Isa 45.7, KJV). Amos 3.6 rhetorically asks, "If a calamity occurs in a city has not Yahweh done it?" The Bible even says that Yahweh will not let the righteous go hungry (Prov. 10.3) and that they will be rewarded with prosperity (Prov. 13.29). Misfortune, on the other hand, is punishment from Yahweh. This is not always the case, but there's no denying Yahweh's active role in earthly suffering and wellbeing in the Bible.

GOD DID IT

Why did we lose the battle? Why did we win the battle? Why were we conquered? Why were we liberated? Why are we suffering from plague, drought, and starvation? Why are our trees bearing such plentiful fruit? Why do certain women miscarry? Why did wild animals eat our kids and our cattle? Well, Yahweh did say that he "will let loose among you the beasts of the field, which will bereave you of your children and destroy your cattle" (Lev. 26.22). This is the worldview in which ancient Near Eastern people interpreted events.

Christians today are still inclined to attribute some events to divine intervention, but often do so inconsistently and uncritically. Believers, for example, are quick to credit God for their personal good fortune. Even in the wake of an unwelcome event, the believer might speculate how God is using it to her advantage, reasoning that *Somehow this is part of God's plan for me,* or *Everything happens for a reason,* or *In the long run, something good will come of this.* I suspect this is not just a Christian tendency, but a human one. Maybe this is healthy optimism, but it might also be a bit self-centered. I can't help but think the credo "everything happens for a reason" would be more accurately expressed as "everything happens to *me* for a reason."

A couple credits God for their conceiving a child, but not for some distant pregnancy resulting from rape. Does God orchestrate conception or not? Does he sometimes use drunken frat parties as a means to bring sperm and egg together, or is such an occurrence simply explained by sinful humans exercising their free will? Pregnancy seems to happen and not happen regardless of whether you are a street kid on heroin or a devout Bible-reading Christian. Many modern believers conveniently shift from one foot to the other — from "it's part of God's plan" to "God gave sinful humans free will."

Families might pray before a meal, thanking God for their food, but never think to attribute starvation to God's doing (and certainly never view hunger and famine as a punishment from God). Does God dole out the food or not? Has he chosen to bless your family with full cupboards, but withhold food from others? Of course not. God doesn't use starvation to punish people. Well actually the God of the Bible does use starvation to punish people. In Amos 4.6, Yahweh tells his people "I gave you also cleanness of teeth in all your cities and lack of bread in all your places" ("cleanness of teeth" is an expression alluding to famine). During the reign of King David, Yahweh used famine to punish the people for something the previous king had done (2 Sam. 21.1). *Eerdmans Commentary on the Bible* states, "famine was always interpreted as a divine punishment."[7] Do Christians still believe that God causes famine? Granted God isn't as vocal as he was in biblical times, so it's hard to know for sure what he's up to. But he does have a strong track record of directly causing famine. Is anyone ready to assert that recent famines in Africa, for example, might be God's inflicting punishment on men, women, and children? Do Christians still believe in this kind of

---

[7] Graeme Auld, "2 Samuel," *Eerdman's Commentary on the Bible*, edited by James D.G. Dunn and John W. Rogerson (Grand Rapids: Eerdmans, 2003), 241.

God?

What about plague and sickness? This is another tool the biblical God uses, as did other ancient Near Eastern gods, to punish humans. "The anger of Yahweh was kindled against the people, and Yahweh struck the people with a very severe plague" (Num. 11.33). These plagues could be nasty: "This will be the plague with which Yahweh will strike all the peoples who have gone to war against Jerusalem; their flesh will rot while they stand on their feet, and their eyes will rot in their sockets, and their tongue will rot in their mouth" (Zech. 14.12). In another instance Yahweh incited King David to count the people of Israel and Judah. David subsequently realized this was a bad thing to do. He repented, asking Yahweh's forgiveness for what he had done (take a census of his people, as Yahweh incited him to do). Ignoring David's plea, Yahweh struck viciously, killing 70,000 of David's people with a plague. A seer named Gad, who passed messages from Yahweh to King David, informed the king that he was to build an altar and sacrifice animals to Yahweh. David did and the plague stopped (2 Sam. 24). Did the Christian God really send horrible, indiscriminate plagues as punishments, or was this just how our ancestors interpreted events?

Fourteenth century Europeans widely believed that the Black Death, which was decimating their population, was God's wrath. In line with biblical thinking, they hypothesized reasons for God's fierce anger and ways to placate the wrathful deity. But now that we have a better understanding of disease, I doubt many modern Christians uphold this interpretation. It would be quite coincidental if the relenting of God's lethal wrath happened to be directly correlated with improvements in sanitation and public health practices through the centuries.

Puritans brought this biblical reasoning to the New World. As the native population was decimated by European disease, John Winthrop saw God's providence: "If God were not pleased with our inheriting these parts, why did he drive out the natives before us? And why dothe he still make roome for us, by deminishinge them as we increase?"[8] Plymouth Colony governor William Bradford biblically reasoned that "It pleased God to visit these Indians with a great sickness."[9] Disease appeared to pass over the Christian settlers while striking down the American Indians. The apparent selective nature of this disease was a clear sign that God was against these pagan natives. After all, this assumption is consistent with God's behavior in the Bible. Yahweh wanted them dead. This biblical belief had consequences.

Are Christians today ready to attribute sickness and disease to divine punishment? Again, I think we find inconsistency. No one seems to ask what sins might have brought on a friend or family member's cancer. Suggesting that God is afflicting a child with cancer is, thankfully, unpalatable today. Generally, God is no longer credited with striking people down with disease, but if a patient recovers, God often gets the credit.

That being said, the biblical worldview isn't totally passé. The notorious Westboro Baptist Church is unabashedly eager to "Thank God for AIDS" at any chance they get.[10] This is God's righteous judgment on gay people. But the Westboro Baptist Church isn't entirely alone on this one. Jerry Falwell, founder of Liberty University — today's largest Christian university, agreed that AIDS is the wrath of God on homosexuals and the societies that tolerate them. And given his commitment to the Bible, it's hard to blame him. In 2013, the Public Religion Research Institute found that 14% of Americans agree with the idea that "AIDS might be God's punishment for immoral sexual behavior."[11] I imagine linking AIDS with God's wrath elicits

---

[8] John Winthrop, *Winthrop Papers*, Vol. 3, (Massachusetts Historical Society, 1943), 149.

[9] Quoted in David Stannard, American Holocaust (New York: Oxford, 1992), 238.

[10] See www.godhatesfags.com

[11] This is down considerably from 1992 when 36% of Americans believed AIDS might be divine punishment. This change correlates well with changing attitudes towards homosexuality. Daniel Cox, Juhem Navarro-Rivera, and Robert P. Jones, "A Shifting Landscape," February 26, 2014, https://www.prri.org/research/2014-lgbt-survey/, (May 25, 2017).

much higher percentages than would other diseases. Does anyone think smallpox or malaria or cancer was sent by God? Bible believers should at least have an open mind on these questions, yet modern Christians appear increasingly uncomfortable with an ancient God.

WAR GOD

Perhaps Yahweh's most conspicuous attribute in the Bible is his proclivity for extreme violence. As Old Testament scholar Peter Enns points out, "Violence seems to be God's preferred method of conflict resolution."[12] In the ancient Near East war was common, and the gods were believed to be instrumental in a nation's success or defeat.

The modest kingdoms of Israel and Judah had the misfortune of existing in the midst of such superpowers as the Egyptians, the Assyrians, the Babylonians, and the Persians. A historian has no need to invoke supernatural intervention to explain Israel's and Judah's perennial struggles. Given their geography their plight is no surprise. But in the Bible, Yahweh is constantly punishing them or rewarding them by moving the region's nations like chess pieces. Yahweh used the mighty Assyrians, for example, to brutalize Israel for their disobedience, and then, eventually, punished the Assyrians for what they had done to Israel.

This conception of gods and war was commonplace and is paralleled in the writings of other ancient Near Eastern peoples. For example, Moab, Israel's neighbor, also had a national god, Chemosh, who directed their war efforts. Israel and Moab fought, as neighboring peoples have tended to do. Sometimes Israel had the upper hand, sometimes Moab did. A Moabite stele, said to be written by "Mesha, son of Chemosh, king of Moab," records Moab's triumphs and struggles.[13] But unlike the

---

[12] Peter Enns, *The Bible Tells Me So: Why Defending Scripture Has Made Us Unable to Read It* (New York: HarperCollins, 2014), 30.

[13] Harper Collins Bible Dictionary, 1996 ed., s.v. "Moabite Stone," by P. Kyle McCarter Jr.

Bible, it interprets events as resulting from the will of Chemosh, not Yahweh. From the Moabite perspective, the reason why Israel oppressed Moab for many years was because Chemosh was angry with his people. But under Mesha's rule, Chemosh brought destruction to Israel. This is biblical thinking, but centered around the god next door.

Of course it's possible that Yahweh actually was directing the geopolitics of the ancient Near East. Sure, all the nations *thought* their gods were in charge, but in reality all were mistaken, except the Israelites. That's possible, but is it plausible? Let's evaluate Yahweh's behavior in the Bible. Is this really the one true God Christians believe in, or an ancient tribal god who behaves how ancient people thought gods behaved?

While this ancient view does make for a powerful deity, it has other implications as well. By using war as an instrument to carry out his will, Yahweh takes credit for some unconscionable crimes. Sometimes Yahweh goes after his enemies' children: "I will sell your sons and your daughters into the hand of the sons of Judah, and they will sell them to the Sabeans, to a distant nation,' for Yahweh has spoken" (Joel 3.8). Selling off people's children to distant nations is cruel, if not ungodly.

Yahweh often has children murdered. "Yahweh our God delivered him over to us, and we . . . utterly destroyed the men, women and children of every city. We left no survivor. We took only the animals as our booty" (Deut. 2.33-35). In Ezekiel 9.6 God says, "Utterly slay old men, young men, maidens, little children, and women." And later we find, "For thus says the Lord God, 'Bring up a company against them and give them over to terror and plunder . . . they will slay their sons and their daughters and burn their houses with fire'" (Ezek 23.46-47). This is the Christian God? Certainly some behaviors can be safely deemed incompatible with God the loving father.

Is indiscriminately slaying men, women, and children necessary? If God is all-powerful and really needs to thin out a population, is there not a less sadistic way to operate? Must children face the harrowing terror of being hacked up by swords? This is disgusting. Hector Avalos points out that since

Yahweh was thought to cause sterility in women, he "could have sterilized Canaanite women supernaturally, and the problem would be solved in a generation or two."[14] Or, if Yahweh really needed the children dead, he could have made them quietly pass away in their sleep. Instead, we read, "How blessed will be the one who seizes and dashes your little ones against the rock" (Ps. 137.9).

Selling kids, slaughtering kids — how heinously must Yahweh act to convince believers that they're on the wrong track? It gets worse. In Isaiah 13, God warns that "the day of Yahweh is coming, cruel, with fury and burning anger." God adds rape to the list of his punishments: "Anyone who is captured will fall by the sword. Their little ones also will be dashed to pieces before their eyes; Their houses will be plundered and their wives ravished." Yahweh continues to explain Babylon's fate: "I am going to stir up the Medes against them . . . their bows will mow down the young men, they will not even have compassion on the fruit of the womb."

In case the phrase "fruit of the womb" wasn't explicit enough, let's look at Hosea 13.16: "Samaria will be held guilty, for she has rebelled against her God. They will fall by the sword, Their little ones will be dashed in pieces, And their pregnant women will be ripped open." And in Hosea 9.16 we find, "They will bear no fruit. Even though they bear children, I will slay the precious ones of their womb." This is how the God of the Bible operates. Once again, what makes more sense, that a loving God was supernaturally moving empires and nations against each other to savagely punish men, pregnant women, and children, or that these events were the result of ancient peoples with ancient theology struggling for power in an ancient barbaric world. I think the answer is painfully obvious.

Let's consider one more example from the Bible. After the Israelites had escaped from bondage in Egypt, the Bible reports that they were attacked by the Amalekites, one of the various peoples that inhabited that region. Moses, with his brother

---

[14] John W. Loftus, ed., *The Christian Delusion* (Amherst, NY: Prometheus, 225.

Aaron and friend Hur, watched the battle from a nearby hilltop. They soon discovered that when Moses raised his hands in the air, Israel would take control of the battle. When he lowered his hands, the Amalekites took control. So, Moses kept his hands in the air. As he tired, Aaron and Hur stepped in to hold up his hands until the Israelites finally defeated the Amalekites (Exod. 17.8-13). But Yahweh was not done with the Amalekites.

About 250 years later, Yahweh decided it was time for King Saul to seek revenge against the Amalekites for their actions 250 years prior. God said, "I will punish Amalek for what he did to Israel, how he set himself against him on the way while he was coming up from Egypt" (1 Sam. 15.2). Fortunately modern countries don't share Yahweh's logic. Imagine Spain, angered by what Napoleon did some 200 years ago, attacking France today, or the United States, upset about the War of 1812, deciding the time is right to seek revenge against the British.

Yahweh continues, "Now go and strike Amalek and utterly destroy all that he has, and do not spare him; but put to death both man and woman, child and infant, ox and sheep, camel and donkey" (1 Sam. 15.3). Yahweh demands that all the men, women, and babies must be butchered for what their ancestors did 250 years earlier. Even the animals must be punished. King Saul carried out these orders . . . well almost. He did kill all the men, women, and children, but he spared the best animals to sacrifice to Yahweh, and took the Amalekite king, Agag, captive. Yahweh was very disappointed that Saul did not kill everything and he regretted that he had ever made Saul king. So Samuel, a prophet of Yahweh, did what Saul failed to do and "hewed Agag in pieces before Yahweh."

Consistently, we see irrational, indiscriminate, savage violence directed by the Christian God, Yahweh, who behaves just as gods used to behave. The Bible set an unfortunate precedent for future generations.

Participants in the Crusades, the Inquisition, witch hunts, the slaughter of Native Americans, and the institution of slavery believed their actions were backed by the God of the Bible. To be fair, believing that God caused and condoned the violent acts recorded in scripture does not mean that he condones every violent act committed in his name. Of course not. People throughout history (and the modern world) have been mistaken about what they think their God is communicating to them. But how does the Christian know which seemingly ungodly acts are from God? Did Yahweh see to the gruesome destruction of the Pequot tribe? Christian soldiers sure thought so.[15] John Underhill, one of the leaders of the Mystic River massacre of the Pequots explained the massacre's religious justification:

> Should not Christians have more mercy and compassion? But I would refer you to David's war. When a people is grown to such a height of blood, and sin against God and man . . . he [God] hath no respect to persons, but harrows them, and saws them, and puts them to the sword, and the most terriblest death that may be. Sometimes the Scriptures declareth women and children must perish with their parents. . . . We have sufficient light from the Word of God for our proceedings."[16]

One can argue that the devout Christian settlers were mistaken about God's will, but one cannot say such barbarity is inconsistent with Yahweh's character. If the believer thinks linking God with ghastly bloodshed is outrageous, maybe he should apply the same outrage and skepticism to the ghastly claims made by the biblical authors.

After the attacks of September 11th Jerry Falwell and Pat Robertson blamed "the pagans and the abortionists and the feminists and the gays and lesbians" of America for the attacks. "God won't be mocked," Falwell said. The two prominent Christians received tremendous blowback for these comments, but we have to admit that their theory is entirely plausible in a biblical worldview. After all, "If a calamity occurs in a city has not Yahweh done it?" (Amos 3.6). Christians must decide if they really believe in this kind of God.

---

[15] Stannard, 111.

[16] Quoted in Eric A. Seibert, *The Violence of Scripture* (Minneapolis: Fortress Press, 2012), 2.

Again, the point of exposing this barbarity is not to bash the Bible, but the belief that it is inspired by God. Christian apologist Paul Copan admits that for believers, "these Yahweh-war texts will certainly prove troubling."[17] His book attempts to exonerate Yahweh from what many see as obvious immorality. First he argues that the extent of the divinely ordained killing in the Bible is exaggerated.[18] Talk of total destruction needs to be viewed in light of the conventional warfare rhetoric of the day. By incorporating this ancient Near Eastern "bravado," the argument goes, God was just trying to speak their language. So when God said, "kill all the men, women, and children," he didn't actually mean *all*, he meant *just give them a good whoopin'*. There's little doubt that the biblical authors did indeed exaggerate these conquests, and other nations did too, but this still doesn't get Yahweh off the hook.

Copan wants his readers to believe that phrases such as "men, women, and children," were just stock phrases that probably excluded noncombatants.[19] In other words, killing "men, women and children" actually means killing soldiers. This isn't convincing at all. Sometimes you have to admit that the Bible means what it says. It's true the women are sometimes kept alive as war spoil and booty for the soldiers (more on this later), but we've already seen verses that specifically mention slaying sons, daughters, and young children; dashing little ones to pieces; plundering houses and ravishing wives; and slaying precious ones of the womb. Saying the violence was restricted to soldiers is a desperate move, one that tacitly admits how immoral the Yahweh character is if the text actually means what it says.

These verses are undeniably challenging to the believer, and it's no surprise apologists will go to great lengths to rationalize them. But remember, we have a perfectly obvious

---

[17] Copan, 188.

[18] Ibid., 170-171.

[19] Ibid., 175-177.

explanation for them: they were written by ancient human beings.

SLAVERY

If the Bible is the best moral book ever, one would expect it to be unmistakably opposed to slavery. Instead, slavery's acceptability is assumed throughout the Bible. The Ten Commandments warn of coveting your neighbor's slaves and other possessions. Yahweh "greatly blessed" Abraham with male and female slaves. Through a curse, God even destined an entire people to be slaves. If Yahweh were opposed to slavery he wouldn't bless people by giving them slaves or sentence a people-group to slavery. But again, this is how ancient people thought, and by extension, their gods behaved.

Given that it's impossible to argue in good faith that the Bible is opposed to slavery, the most common defense of the Bible's moral failure is that the slavery it describes isn't that bad. We moderns automatically picture the kind of slavery practiced in the American South, which Christian apologists make clear was despicably immoral and much different from the kind that God greenlighted in the Bible. The first thing to point out with this line of defense is that it doesn't make the case that biblical slavery is good or moral; it just argues that it's different and not that bad. Well, let's see...

Exhibit number one for the Christian apologist is invariably this: "When you buy a male Hebrew slave, he shall serve six years, but in the seventh he shall go out a free person" (Exod. 21.2). The Bible calls for a mere six years of service. There is no denying that temporary slavery is better than perpetual slavery. Copan explains the practicality and the mildness of biblical slavery: "an Israelite strapped for shekels might become an indentured servant to pay off his debt. . . . this servanthood wasn't much different *experientially* from paid employment in a cash economy like ours."[20] He even offers up this comparison:

---

[20] Copan, 125.

"Think of a sports player today who gets 'traded' to another team, to which he 'belongs.' Yes, teams have 'owners,' but we're hardly talking about slavery here!"

Was this slavery really as benign as Copan wants us to believe? Let's continue reading from Exodus 21 to see how closely this kind of slavery resembles a modern job in which a worker earns money and then pays off student loans and credit card debt: "If his master gives him a wife and she bears him sons or daughters, the wife and her children shall be her master's and he shall go out alone." Ooh, there's a minor difference. Allow me to reiterate. If the master provides a wife for the slave (or Copan might prefer "employee"), the master gets to keep the slave's wife and kids after his six-year service is up.

A few verses later, we find this: "When a man sells his daughter as a slave, she shall not go out as the male slaves do." In other words, she is not released after six years, but remains a slave indefinitely. And a few verses after that we read, "If a man strikes his male or female slave with a rod and he dies at his hand, he shall be punished. If, however, he survives a day or two, no vengeance shall be taken; for he is his property." This verse regulates how severely a master can beat his slave, and, according to the Bible, slaves, both men and women, may be beaten to death as long as they don't die within a day or two of the beating. To be fair, a few verses later it does say that if a slave owner destroys a slave's eye or tooth, then he must set the slave free. But still, the Bible is clear that harsh beatings *are* acceptable. The Bible even tells us *why* masters can beat their slaves: because the slave is "his property."[21]

Sadly, apologists try to spin these verses as a positive,

---

[21] The Hebrew word translated as *property,* can be translated as *money* or *silver,* but the point is the same. Some argue that this verse does not mean the slave is the master's property, but that harshly beating a slave will impact the master's *money* (loss of productivity, maybe some doctor bills). This natural financial consequence of beating the slave apparently somehow excuses the master's behavior. I wonder if a modern boss could beat an employee to an inch of her life and avoid punishment with this defense.

flaunting the "strict rules" governing a slave's treatment.[22] I don't think they realize there were, at times, similar restraints put on southern slave owners.[23] For example, Louisiana law stated, "The slave is entirely subject to the will of his master, who may correct and chastise him, though not with unusual rigor, nor so as to maim or mutilate him, or to expose him to the danger of loss of life, or to cause his death."[24] Unlike the statute in Leviticus, this one does not permit a master to kill his slave.

So is biblical slavery an approximate moral equivalent to "paid employment in a cash economy like ours"? Not even close. We might be required to get jobs to pay debt obligations today, but our employers cannot legally beat us to death or assume ownership of our kids.

If the temporary nature of Hebrew slavery is supposed to be the key moral distinction that elevates it high above southern slavery, Christians have a big problem. Only male *Israelite* slaves are to be released after six years. As for foreign slaves, Yahweh is very clear:

> As for the male and female slaves whom you may have, it is from the nations around you that you may acquire male and female slaves. You may also acquire them from among the aliens residing with you, and from their families that are with you, who have been born in your land; and they may be your property. You may keep them as a possession for your children after you, for them to inherit as property. These you may treat as slaves, but as for your fellow Israelites, no one shall rule over the other with harshness (Lev. 25.44-46 NRSV).

Verses like this should make obvious to everyone the danger of preserving ancient social norms as the "word of God." In 1860, when abolitionists labeled slavery a sin, Rev. Henry J. Van Dyke cited these verses, "plainly written in the divine law," as he

---

[22] Walter C. Kaiser Jr. et al., Hard Sayings of the Bible (Downers Grove, IL: InterVarsity, 1996), 149.

[23] Regulation or lack thereof varied by state and era.

[24] Civil code of Louisiana, Article 173.

admonished them for blaspheming "the name of God and his doctrine."[25] Yahweh condones slavery, pure and simple: "You may keep them as a possession for your children after you, for them to inherit as property. These you may treat as slaves." If Christian apologists are so vehemently opposed to the slavery of the antebellum South, one wonders how they can possibly turn around and embrace the morality of biblical slavery. The Bible allows for slaves to be beaten, bought, sold, owned forever, and passed down to future generations.

Some might argue that slavery was just too entrenched for God to root out at that time and place in history. Well, God definitely entrenched it even more. And does anybody really believe this is the best God could do? Copan argues that the Bible's slavery is superior to the slavery of other ancient cultures. OK. That's a pretty low and fuzzy bar to set for God. Could God not do any better than, "When a man sells his daughter as a slave, she shall not go out as the male slaves do"? The much older Babylonian Code of Hammurabi outdoes Yahweh with this parallel: "If a destitute father of a household sells his wife, his son, or his daughter into slavery to pay a debt, then the creditor cannot keep them as slaves for more than three years and must free them at the beginning of the fourth year" (117). If this verse were in the Bible, apologists would be celebrating its moral superiority. But the apologists are stuck with what they were given by the Bible's ancient authors. The Bible got slavery wrong, but for the apologist, the Bible is not allowed to be wrong.

Some might want to argue that slavery is just another Old Testament oddity to be ignored, but the New Testament does little to negate the Old Testament position. In fact, it consistently instructs slaves to accept their status and obey their masters.[26]

---

25 Henry J. Van Dyke, "The Character and Influence of Abolitionism," in *Fast Day Sermons; or The Pulpit on the State of the Country* (New York: Rudd and Carleton, 1861), 139.

26 See 1 Pet. 2.18, Eph. 6.5, Col. 3.22, 1 Tim., 6.1, Cor. 7.21. Jesus also builds parables around slavery, see Luke 12.41-48.

One might argue that the New Testament authors were covertly opposed to slavery, they just chose not to confront it because doing so would detract from the primary mission of saving souls. That's logically possible. This new sect was already seen as subversive in many ways; the last thing they needed was to wage war on a thoroughly entrenched practice. The apostle Paul carried the message that all were equal before God, regardless of current social status. So in effect, one might argue, Paul *was* subtly fighting slavery by changing people's hearts.

Paul urged slaves to be obedient but he also encouraged good behavior from slave masters. One hopes Paul's instruction has softened some slave masters through the centuries, but by issuing such guidance, Paul effectively canonized the existence and normality of the slave/master relationship. For Paul, one's status in this life is irrelevant: "Only, as the Lord has assigned to each one, as God has called each, in this manner let him walk. . . . Were you called while a slave? Do not worry about it . . . Brethren, each one is to remain with God in that condition in which he was called" (1 Cor. 7.17-24). The New Testament's countenance of slavery might stem from the authors' mistaken belief that this world would shortly pass away. Best focus on the next life rather than polishing brass on a sinking ship. Or it could have been accepted simply because it was the norm, and because God so clearly endorsed it in their scriptures. Whatever the reason, here we are 2,000 years later. Countless humans have been robbed of life and liberty and the Bible has too easily validated the continuation of slavery. The New Testament never condemns slavery, instead it urges slaves to accept their servitude.

Some defend the Bible by pointing out that its overarching message is one of love and compassion. For example Leviticus 19.33-34 reads, "When a stranger resides with you in your land, you shall not do him wrong. The stranger who resides with you shall be to you as the native among you, and you shall love him as yourself." This is nice, but it doesn't erase Yahweh's endorsement of slavery. It only shows that, like humans throughout history, Yahweh hasn't worked through his morality in a consistent way. The Babylonian king, Hammurabi, was called by the gods "to prevent the strong from oppressing the weak" and "promote the welfare of mankind."[27] Can we then conclude that the Code of Hammurabi doesn't really mean what it says concerning slavery? A few thousand years later, the American Revolution was celebrating the virtues of liberty and equality with no intention of ending slavery or allowing women to vote. The nice verses in the Bible don't cancel out the ones that clearly teach that humans can be bought, sold, beaten, and inherited.

Some argue that all the foreign slaves were prisoners of war and so they would require harsh treatment at times. Conquered combatants could pose a threat to peace and order. With too much freedom they might orchestrate revolt. But the Bible flatly condones owning people as property and never instructs that slaves must be enemy combatants. These lifelong slaves were simply foreigners, even "aliens residing with you, and from their families that are with you, who have been born in your land" (Lev. 25.45). But, while we're on the topic of prisoners of war, let's explore.

"TO THE VICTOR BELONG THE SPOILS"

The Bible tells us that after the Flood, Noah planted a vineyard and made wine. One day he drank too much and passed out naked in his tent. His son Ham saw him. The Bible is short on details here, but it's possible Ham made some jokes about his naked and intoxicated dad. Noah's two other (more respectful) sons, Shem and Japheth, carefully covered their exposed father with a blanket, their faces "turned away, so that they did not see their father's nakedness."

When Noah awoke he was furious with Ham, but instead of punishing Ham, Noah cursed one of Ham's kids, Canaan: "Cursed be Canaan; lowest of slaves shall he be to his brothers."

---

[27] Davies W. W. The Codes of Hammurabi and Moses (Cincinnati: Jennings and Graham, 1905), 17.

The curse then spells out that Shem and Japheth will be blessed by Yahweh, and Canaan will be their slave (Gen. 9.20-27). In the Bible the entire human population fans out from Noah's family members, so this is no small curse. God and Noah are setting the future world order.

(This story was used to justify black slavery in the South. Benjamin Palmer, a prominent minister and theologian of the 19th century American South expressed this common sentiment: "The outspreading landscape of all history is embraced within the camera of Noah's brief prophecy; showing how from the beginning God not only distributed them upon the face of the earth, but impressed upon each branch the type of character fitting it for its mission."[28] If God did indeed mark a particular branch of people for slavery, and if black Africans were now the ones enslaved, then, by the reasoning of many in the 19th century, black Africans must be the descendants of Canaan. According to the Bible, slavery was the natural position of Canaan's descendants. Christian slave owners had a Christian duty to steward and Christianize this heathen population whom God marked for servitude.)

But why did God and Noah issue such a horrible curse? And why did God and Noah curse Canaan, Ham's son, instead of Ham, the allegedly guilty party? The reason is that the cursing of Canaan serves as a backstory, retrojected into the text. It is meant, however ridiculously, to explain and justify an event that takes place later in the Bible: the Israelites' conquest of the Canaanites (the descendants of Canaan).

Just prior to this conquest, in the book of Deuteronomy, Yahweh provides instruction to his people before they invade. The people of Canaan are to be killed or enslaved:

> When you draw near to a town to fight against it, offer it terms of peace. If it accepts your terms of peace and surrenders to you, **then all the people in it shall serve you at forced labor.** If it does

---

[28] Stephen R. Haynes, Noah's Curse: The Biblical Justification of American Slavery (New York: Oxford, 2002), 133.

not submit to you peacefully, but makes war against you, then you shall besiege it; and when Yahweh your God gives it into your hand, you shall put all its males to the sword. You may, however, **take as your booty the women, the children, livestock, and everything else in the town, all its spoil. You may enjoy the spoil of your enemies, which Yahweh your God has given you** (Deut. 20.10-15).

This is repugnant. Taking women as the spoils of war was common practice a long time ago, but again, this is the Bible, God's word, the purported foundation of goodness.

Remember, a common apologetic is to argue biblical slavery was necessary in order to subdue the defeated enemy combatants, but this isn't the story told in the Bible. Here we see God ordering the slaughter of all the males and the surviving women and children were considered "booty," a prize of sorts. They and their descendents could be owned and passed down for generations.

Apologists try their hardest to spin this dreadful passage into a humanitarian one. Copan claims that "rather than being outcasts" these women now have the chance to get married and integrate into Israelite society as equals.[29] Again, Copan feels the need to help the Bible out, massaging and supplementing the text. Just read the passage again: "Take as your booty the women, the children, livestock, and everything else in the town, all its spoil. You may enjoy the spoil of your enemies." If one lets the Bible speak for itself, one will see that this passage is about the spoils of war, not the wellbeing of women, children, and livestock.

Here's another troubling text: "Kill every male among the little ones, and kill every woman who has known man intimately. But all the girls who have not known man intimately, spare for yourselves . . . Now the booty that remained from the spoil which the men of war had plundered was 675,000 sheep, and 72,000 cattle, and 61,000 donkeys, and of human beings, of

---

[29] Copan, 121.

the women who had not known man intimately, all the persons were 32,000" (Num. 31.17-18, 33-35). There must be some point at which defending this stuff is just too tasteless to stomach.

IS GOD SEXIST? YAHWEH IS.

> *"And if you say in your heart, 'Why have these things come upon me?' it is for the greatness of your iniquity that your skirts are lifted up, and you are violated. . . . I myself will lift up your skirts over your face, and your shame will be seen"* (Jer. 13.22, 26 NRSV).

Lifting up skirts to enable violation? One could argue over how literally Yahweh should be taken here, but in any case, is this how God talks? Creepy.

> *"When the house of Israel lived on their own soil, they defiled it with their ways and their deeds; their conduct in my sight was like the uncleanness of a woman in her menstrual period. So I poured out my wrath upon them"* (Ezek. 36.17-18 NRSV).

Is this how the creator of the universe talks? Is he so disgusted with a woman on her period?

Throughout the Old Testament, Yahweh is depicted as the husband, and Israel the wife. In this marriage metaphor, Israel is often accused of cheating, that is, worshipping other gods:

> *Therefore, O whore, hear the word of the Lord: Thus says the Lord God, Because your lust was poured out and your nakedness uncovered in your whoring with your lovers . . . I will gather all your lovers, with whom you took pleasure . . . and will uncover your nakedness to them, so that they may see all your nakedness. **I will judge you as women who commit adultery** and shed blood are judged, **and bring blood upon you in wrath and jealousy.** I will deliver you into their hands, . . . **they shall strip you of your clothes** and take your beautiful objects and leave you naked and bare. They*

*shall bring up a mob against you, and **they shall stone you and cut you to pieces with their swords**. They shall burn your houses and execute judgments on you in the sight of many women; **I will stop you from playing the whore** . . . So **I will satisfy my fury on you**, and my jealousy shall turn away from you; I will be calm, and will be angry no longer* (Ezek. 16.35-42 NRSV).

Is this how God talks? That Yahweh would model this kind of violence in response to an unfaithful wife is unfortunate, to say the least. Old Testament professor Eric Seibert laments that "God is portrayed as an abusive husband who sexually degrades and humiliates his wife (Israel). . . . [This] is not a healthy picture of marriage but a horrifying depiction of spousal abuse."[30]

And while we're on the topic of jealous husbands . . . "When a spirit of jealousy comes over a man and he is jealous of his wife, he shall then make the woman stand before Yahweh." The woman is then subjected to a trial by ordeal. Trials by ordeal, which have been common in various superstitious cultures, subjected the accused to an unpleasant experience as a way of determining guilt or innocence. For example, in the Code of Hammurabi a woman suspected of adultery is tried in the river. If she drowns she is guilty, if she survives she is innocent (132). In the Bible a woman suspected of adultery must drink the "water of bitterness that brings a curse," which is a mix of holy water and floor scrapings. If she is immune to the water of bitterness, she is innocent. But if she is guilty the concoction will make her "abdomen swell" and her "thigh waste away" (Num. 5.11-31). Men didn't have to worry about being subjected to these tests.

THE NEW TESTAMENT IS OLD, TOO

Does the New Testament liberate women from the Old Testament? It does reveal that there were women who played important roles in some of the early churches. Additionally Paul

---

[30] Seibert, 137.

authored this radical statement: "There is neither Jew nor Greek, there is neither slave nor free man, there is neither male nor female; for you are all one in Christ Jesus" (Gal. 3.28). Yet Paul also gave us statements such as, "The women are to keep silent in the churches; for they are not permitted to speak, but are to subject themselves, just as the Law also says. If they desire to learn anything, let them ask their own husbands at home; for it is improper for a woman to speak in church" (1 Cor. 14.34-35).

Many scholars believe that the latter statement, along with other texts that subordinate women in the New Testament, was not actually written by Paul, but forged after his death. If this is true, later, more traditional (sexist) voices writing in his name attempted to dampen his progressive message. If these texts were *not* interpolations and forgeries, but were indeed original to Paul, then we can conclude that Paul is not the modern man we had hoped he was, and Galatians 3.28 (There is neither male nor female in Christ) must be interpreted in light of this.

Both possibilities are problematic for the Bible. First, it's worth pointing out that even *if* the New Testament did somehow rescind the blatant sexism of the Old Testament, this would not erase Yahweh's checkered past. But the fact remains that the New Testament has its fair share of sexist verses too. Even if the sexist bits were not written by Paul, they have still been deemed holy scripture, and have therefore influenced social attitudes through the centuries. (This possibility also opens up a fresh can of worms: the Bible contains forgeries.) If Paul *did* write the sexist verses, this sharply limits the degree to which we can read Paul's Galatians verse as advocating the liberation of women.

As we've seen with slavery, Paul did not attempt to undo the social order. He reinforced the social order. So, when Paul states that "in Christ" there is "neither male nor female," he means male and female souls are of equal value before God. One's earthly status will ultimately not matter. In the end the only relevant categories are Christian and non-Christian, saved and unsaved — but down here on earth, in this life, women are subordinate to men. And this becomes clear as we widen our scope.

To the dismay of many, the subordination of women is baked into the Christian cake. God subordinated females early on. Because of Eve's disobedience in the Garden, Yahweh declared, "I will greatly multiply your pain in childbirth, In pain you will bring forth children; yet your desire will be for your husband, and he will rule over you" (Gen. 3). In this foundational text, we see that God's curse is the reason husbands rule over their wives (and childbirth is so painful).

The New Testament expands on the sexism that the Old Testament legitimized:

> Let a woman learn in silence with full submission. I permit no woman to teach or to have authority over a man; she is to keep silent. For Adam was formed first, then Eve; and Adam was not deceived, but the woman was deceived and became a transgressor. Yet she will be saved through childbearing (1 Tim. 2.11-15).

Most scholars believe this letter, 1 Timothy, is a forgery (not actually written by Paul, who the author claims to be), but regardless, it is holy scripture. A woman is not permitted to have authority over a man. By grounding his claim in the creation of man and woman, the author makes a sweeping pronouncement about a woman's place. He reasons that women are, by nature, easily deceived, which can lead to some very bad things. Remember the Fall? Eve literally ruined everything. But, the author strangely adds, a woman can be "saved through childbearing."

In 1 Corinthians we find, "Christ is the head of every man, and the man is the head of a woman, and God is the head of Christ" (11.3) A few verses later we read, "[Man] is the image and glory of God; but the woman is the glory of man. For man does not originate from woman, but woman from man; for indeed man was not created for the woman's sake, but woman for the man's sake" (11.7-9). Again, we see the New Testament grounding a woman's subordination in creation. The logic is based on Genesis 2. God removed one of Adam's ribs and fashioned it into "a helper suitable for him." Adam named the new creature "Woman." Because woman came from man, the author declares that "he is the image and glory of God; but the woman is the glory of man." From this ancient understanding of human origins, the New Testament concludes that "man was not created for the woman's sake, but woman for the man's sake." That's quite a dangerous claim from a book that many human beings have long considered the infallible word of God. Women have paid the price for these scriptures.

Happily, most modern Christians find these verses problematic. To make them less problematic apologists must devise creative explanations to soften their "seeming" offensiveness and harmfulness. But airbrushing these verses wasn't necessary until recently — and the reason is simple: these problematic verses were not seen as problematic for the majority of Christian history. Just as Adam and Eve were unproblematic in a prescientific world, the Bible's misogyny was unproblematic in a normatively patriarchal world. The Bible simply wasn't at odds with the culture, in fact, it validated the culture. Remember, women weren't guaranteed the right to vote in the United States until less than 100 years ago. We should not be surprised to find undisguised sexism in a first-century text (unless, of course, one regards the Bible as a divinely inspired book).

When the battle over women's suffrage finally surfaced in the 19th century (1,800 years after the New Testament writings), the Bible was naturally invoked to defend tradition. Are women too easily deceived to be trusted with the vote? Might women use the vote to usurp authority from men? Can a woman vote against her husband? All fair questions if one believes in biblical authority. The Reverend H. M. Goodwin argued that "Woman is made to be the complement and help-mate, not the rival of man. . . . This whole movement for female suffrage, is, at least in its motive and beginning, a rebellion against the divinely ordained position and duties of woman."[31] Even author Susan Fenimore Cooper reminded her fellow Christian women that "Christianity confirms the subordinate position of woman, by allotting to man the headship in plain language."[32] This debate wasn't very long ago. And one can probably imagine that as we back up in time, the situation doesn't get better.

Carla Casagrande, expert in Medieval philosophy, recapitulates the pervasive biblical thinking of the Middle Ages: "The divine curse that accompanied Eve as she fell from Paradise on Earth was echoed in the life of every woman to follow, condemning her irrevocably to the domination of men."[33] At a time when civil society and theology were thoroughly infused, books like 1 Corinthians and 1 Timothy licensed men to control women's attire, behavior, and speech. Going back further, we find no shortage of unenlightened, distasteful, and damaging ideas from Church Fathers. For example, Tertullian, around the year 200, authored "On the Apparel of Women," in which he stated,

> Do you not know that you are (each) an Eve? The sentence of God on this sex of yours lives in this age: the guilt must of necessity live too. You are the devil's gateway: you are the unsealer of that (forbidden) tree: you are the first deserter of the divine law: you are she who persuaded him whom the devil was not valiant enough to attack. You destroyed so easily God's image, man. On account of your desert— that is, death— even the Son of God had to die.

If a modern Christian leader penned these remarks or the scriptures that inspired them, he would be roundly rebuked,

---

[31] Rev. Prof. H. M. Goodwin, "Women's Suffrage," March 1884, Retrieved from http://www.bible-researcher.com/women/suffrage.html (May 26, 2017).

[32] Susan Fenimore Cooper, "Female Suffrage: A Letter to the Christian Women of America," 1870, Retrieved from http://external.oneonta.edu/cooper/susan/suffrage.html (May 26, 2017).

[33] Christiane Klapsich-Zuber, ed., A History of Women: Silences of the Middle Ages (Cambridge, MA: Belknap Press, 1994), 90-99.

shamed, and labeled a pig. But the Bible somehow gets a pass. Again, given the time and place in which the Bible was created, we shouldn't be surprised at its contents. But we should be surprised when Joel Osteen's website reads, "We believe the entire Bible is inspired by God, without error and the authority on which we base our faith, conduct and doctrine."[34]

FEMALES TREATED AS PROPERTY

In the Bible, women are consistently treated as the property of men. Examples are numerous, creating a pattern that cannot be dismissed.

> When you go out to battle against your enemies, and Yahweh your God delivers them into your hands and you take them away captive, and see among the captives a beautiful woman, and have a desire for her and would take her as a wife for yourself, then you shall bring her home to your house, and she shall shave her head and trim her nails. She shall also remove the clothes of her captivity and shall remain in your house, and mourn her father and mother a full month; and after that you may go in to her and be her husband and she shall be your wife. It shall be, if you are not pleased with her, then you shall let her go wherever she wishes; but you shall certainly not sell her for money, you shall not mistreat her, because you have humbled her (Deut. 21.10-14).

Was this written by God? It definitely wasn't written by a woman. The above passage, from Deuteronomy, a book addressed to a male audience from a male deity, explains that soldiers were free to pick out a wife from a conquered population. Nonetheless, Copan tries to celebrate this statute as a protective measure: "She was the one who benefited from this legislation."[35] He touts the one-month "period of reflection" the Bible affords these brides-to-be to mourn the loss of their

---

[34] Joel Osteen Ministries, "What We Believe," https://www.joelosteen.com/Pages/WhatWeBelieve.aspx, (May 26, 2017).
[35] Copan, 120.

parents. He's also impressed by the stipulation that if the man is not pleased with her, he shall let her go free instead of selling her. It is nice that a man is prevented from selling a woman he made his wife (or one of his wives), but again, this is a very low moral bar to clear.

These verses are not about charity. They are about taking a "beautiful woman" that you "have a desire for." If this policy were really meant as a kindhearted safety net for survivors, wouldn't God also provide for the women who did not happen to elicit sexual desire from their conquerors? (These leftovers can be taken as common war booty.) And are these beautiful foreign women supposed to be the lucky ones? (Because what every girl wants is to marry the man who just hacked up her family.) The woman has no say in the matter. Her will is never considered. The fact that she gets a month to mourn before the soldier is free to "go in to her" does not make this OK. Apologists need to stop defending this stuff.

The book of Judges shows similar disregard for females following an episode in which God ordered the Israelites to slaughter their fellow tribe of Benjamin. Benjamin was nearly wiped out, just 600 men remained. The other tribes swore to Yahweh they would not give their daughters to Benjamin as wives. But yet they were concerned that without mates the tribe of Benjamin would die out. Around the same time, the tribe elders realized that the Israelite town of Jabesh-gilead was absent in their war against Benjamin. Instead of contributing, they stayed home. So the elders decided to slaughter the men, women, and children of Jabesh-gilead, but save the virgin girls. Problem solved. They collected 400 virgins from Jabesh-gilead and gave them to the Benjaminites as wives. But they were still 200 short. They wanted enough virgins for all the sons of Benjamin. The elders saw another opportunity in an upcoming festival in Shiloh. During this festival girls would dance out in the open. The wifeless sons of Benjamin were instructed to hide in the vineyards and wait for the girls to come out: "Each of you shall catch his wife from the daughters of Shiloh. . . . The sons of Benjamin did so, and took wives according to their number from those who danced, whom they carried away" (Judg. 21). And the tribe of Benjamin was able to continue breeding.

One could argue that God didn't condone this particular capturing of virgins; the Bible is simply recounting what happened. The problem is that this behavior fits all too comfortably in the Bible. As we've seen, Yahweh's morality is not above this. Moreover, Yahweh once ordered the savage execution of a man for "gathering sticks on the Sabbath" (Num. 15.32). If he thinks picking up sticks is worthy of capital punishment, I would hope he also finds capturing and raping virgin girls worth condemning. But apparently he does not.

The Bible regularly ignores the interests of females. Males distribute females to other males as they see fit. King Saul freely gave away his daughters as wives: "Here is my older daughter Merab; I will give her to you as a wife" (1 Sam 18.17). In true caveman fashion, Samson states, "I saw a woman in Timnah, one of the daughters of the Philistines; now therefore, get her for me as a wife. . . . Get her for me, for she looks good to me" (Judg. 14.2-3). Even Yahweh gives out women: "Therefore I will give their wives to others" (Jer. 8.10). And Yahweh tells King David, 'It is I who anointed you king . . . I also gave you your master's house and your master's wives" (2 Sam. 12.7-8). As we've seen, a father could sell his daughter to another man. The buyer could keep her as a wife, but he could also choose to give her to his son (Exod. 21.7-11). Women were transferred like property.

The Ten Commandments, which are addressed to a male audience,[36] place wives in the list of property: "You shall not covet your neighbor's house; you shall not covet your neighbor's wife or his male servant or his female servant or his ox or his donkey or anything that belongs to your neighbor" (Exod. 20.17). The issue in this commandment is not adultery, per se. Any condemnation of adultery in the Bible only surfaces when another man's property has been violated. Male monogamy was never the issue, as Coogan states, "Adultery was in effect

---

[36] The Hebrew is written in second person masculine. Michael Coogan, *God & Sex* (New York: Twelve, 2010), 102.

expropriation of property."[37]

In the Bible sometimes a maidservant will be called upon to mate with the head of household. Sarah offered up her maidservant to Abraham, as did Rachel and Leah (sisters) to their husband, Jacob. Never are the rights of the maidservant considered; the concern is that the man has sons. Passing out maidservants to masters is mentioned so nonchalantly that a reader could easily miss how sad a picture this is. Imagine if a modern live-in nanny were commanded to provide sons for the head of household. Yahweh could have easily forbidden this practice, but, like an ancient Near Eastern man, he doesn't seem to notice anything disagreeable about it.

Having sons is important to Yahweh. If a woman's husband dies before she can provide him with one, "her husband's brother shall go in to her and take her to himself as wife and perform the duty of a husband's brother to her." The brother is tasked with conceiving a son with his sister-in-law/new wife, "so that his [brother's] name will not be blotted out from Israel" (Deut. 25.5-6). This concept was not unique to Yahweh. The Hittite and Middle Assyrian codes prescribed similar protocol.[38] Did Yahweh borrow patriarchal ideas he liked from neighboring cultures?

The Bible's misogyny is on full display in its laws concerning rape and female virginity. If a man sleeps with or rapes a virgin engaged to another man, he is put to death, but if she is not engaged, we have a different story. If the *unengaged* virgin is "seduced," the man must either marry her or pay the price of a dowry for virgins to the girl's father (Exod. 22.16-17). If she is raped, the rapist must marry her and pay her father the attendant bride price. He is not permitted to divorce her (Deut. 22.28-29). Whether she is raped or seduced matters little in the Bible. Either way, it is the father who is wronged and compensated. The female is completely disregarded. She is

---

[37] Ibid., 102.

[38] Victor H. Matthews and Don C. Benjamin, Old Testament Parallels, 3rd ed. (New York: Paulist Press, 2006), 118, 125.

forever married to her rapist. If she had been engaged, the rapist would be put to death, but in this case the rapist lives. His consequence is that he must marry the girl he raped. What is the moral of this story? That rapists must choose their victims wisely? Not good.

Male virginity is a nonissue in the Bible, but female virginity is of great concern. If a girl is found not to be a virgin on her wedding night, "then they shall bring out the girl to the doorway of her father's house, and the men of her city shall stone her to death" (Deut. 22.20-21). These verses must be unequivocally denounced, not defended.

LET'S NOT PRETEND

In Biola University's statement of faith, we find, "The Scriptures of the Old and New Testaments are without error or misstatement in their moral and spiritual teaching and record of historical facts. They are without error or defect of any kind."[39] Claiming that the Bible is morally, spiritually, and historically perfect makes me scratch my head, hard. But on the other hand, I'm not surprised given what the Bible is believed to be. Perfection is an understandable expectation for a book inspired by the creator of the universe. Why would God inspire mistaken ideas? Why would he inspire anything less than mind-blowing accuracy and first-rate moral guidance? Furthermore, Christianity's foundational doctrines have been painstakingly built from these texts. Accepting these doctrines necessitates a firm belief in the Bible's reliability and inspiration. A fallible Bible shakes the foundations of the faith.

Believers have maintained their commitment to inerrancy through creative reinterpretation, elusion, and chalking up troubling passages to mystery, which they can ask God about in due time. Where there's a will there's a way. But no such acrobatics are necessary to explain the Bible. The contradictions,

---

[39] Biola University Doctrinal Statement, https://www.biola.edu/about/doctrinal-statement, (May 24, 2017).

the inaccuracies, the animal sacrifice, the violence, the slavery, and the sexism are exactly what we would expect from an ancient human text.

Biblical interpretations clearly shift through time to ease the book's dissonance with modern knowledge and culture, but changing the plain meaning of a divinely inspired text is never easy. Debates about a fixed earth, the age of the earth, evolution, slavery, and women's rights have gone hand in hand with debates about biblical inspiration and authority. At this moment in history, we can see biblical interpretation struggling to keep up with culture in debates about same-sex marriage. Evangelical Christianity is slowly making peace with homosexuality despite verses such as Leviticus 20.13: "If there is a man who lies with a male as those who lie with a woman, both of them have committed a detestable act; they shall surely be put to death. Their blood guiltiness is upon them."

7. CONCLUSIÓN

Where did we come from? The Bible teaches that God made us in the beginning, about 6,000 years ago. A couple thousand years after that, God decided to start over. He flooded the earth, killing everyone except a handful of people who were tasked with repopulating the planet. Christianity stopped making sense when science discovered that none of this is true. Theologians have since endeavored to de-literalize the Bible's human origins stories in various ways, but the reality is that Christian theology needs certain pieces to be literally true. Christianity holds that Adam and Eve were created innocent and in communion with God, but these first two humans still managed to wreak havoc. Their disobedience brought sin and death into the world. As their descendants we are now mortal, stained with a corrupted nature, and destined for a very bad place when we die.

Given what science has uncovered about our origins, retaining some form of this story has proved extremely challenging. But its incompatibility with reality should not be surprising. The story of Adam, Eve, and the Fall was a prescientific conception, an ancient guess about our origins, which came to be regarded as the ultimate authority. Christian theology was built upon prescientific ideas. Theologians are trying to put Christianity back together but the old pieces have no place in the puzzle that science has assembled.

Next, we looked at the punishment for not believing Christianity is true: hell. Does eternal conscious torment make sense to most modern Christians? It's a twisted concept, and grossly incompatible with the God that most Christians believe in today. The medieval mind readily believed in and feared a God who subjected sinners to endless and abject horror, but modern Christians don't know what to do with this belief. It has become a doctrine that is held quietly, for it threatens to unmask the groovy God advertised by so many modern evangelical churches. Understandably, there is a strong impulse to soft-pedal or obfuscate such a heinous topic, but trying to soften eternal conscious torment is a ridiculous task. In addition, does it really make sense that God would predicate the avoidance of eternal damnation upon hearing a particular story and believing it to be true? Modern humans have been around for 200,000 years, but this salvific story surfaced just 2,000 years ago in one geographic region? Does it make sense that all the Buddhists, Hindus, Muslims, and Mormons will all spend eternity in hell? Does it make sense that God would make country-of-origin a leading factor in determining one's beliefs, which in turn determine whether one is infinitely punished or not? Does this seem like a system that a rational, loving God would put in place, or one that was cobbled together by ancient humans? Be honest.

Finally, Yahweh is not a God that makes sense to modern people. In fact he's really not the kind of God that most Christian churches believe in today. He's the kind of God that people used to believe in. One might opt to follow Jesus instead of Yahweh, but long ago Christianity decided Yahweh and Jesus are one being. Additionally, both the Old *and* New Testaments promote outdated teachings about science, slavery, and women, to name a few.

The Bible is an undeniably intriguing book, but it is inspired not by a perfect being but by human beings. Is it the kind of book that should embolden someone to oppose modern science? Is it the kind of book that should serve as the grounds for rejecting evolution, or believing that humans used to live to be 900 years old? Is it the kind of book that one can depend upon to know what happens to us after we die? Is it the kind of book one should consult to uncover secrets about the end times? Is it the kind of book that one should read to learn a woman's place in society? Is it the kind of book that should serve as the basis for one's opposition to same-sex marriage? The ancient people who wrote the Bible had ancient ideas. Does it make sense to canonize these ancient ideas as the infallible word of God?

APPENDIX: LIBERAL CHRISTIANITY

While there are a bewildering number of Christian
denominations and churches, most can be broadly categorized as
either theologically liberal or theologically conservative.
Conservative churches, referred to as *evangelical*, *fundamentalist*,
or even *biblical* or *bible-believing*, maintain the traditional
Christian doctrines. These conservative, evangelical,
fundamentalist, biblical Christians believe in the truth and
centrality of the Bible. On the liberal side of the ledger we find
the so-called mainline denominations — denominations with
deep historical roots in the United States, such as the United
Methodist Church, Episcopal Church, and Presbyterian Church.
These denominations historically constituted the majority of
American Christians and were originally theologically similar to
today's conservative churches (which for the most part,
ironically, are non-denominational churches). This divide began
to calcify in the early 20th century when the unrelenting advance
of biblical scholarship, geology, biology, etc. convinced many
within Christendom that certain traditional beliefs were no
longer tenable.

Fearing that Christianity was unraveling, traditionalists
took a stand. In the 1910s, a series of essays published under the
title *The Fundamentals* outlined and defended Christian

orthodoxy. Central to this effort was the belief in the infallibility of the Bible. Modern scholarship was exposing the Bible as a very human book. But if the Bible is just the work of human authors and editors from a distant time and place doing their best to make sense of reality, then there's surely no rational grounds for moderns to base their lives upon it. To be sure, this would not preclude the Bible's ability to offer up some deep truths that speak to the human condition, but at the end of the day, the Bible becomes an interesting historical record of ancient traditions, insights, and speculation about invisible things. Gravely aware of the slippery slope, Rev. Dyson Hague, contributing author of *The Fundamentals*, warned, "If the first chapters of Genesis are unreliable, the revelation of the beginning of the universe, the origin of the race, and the reason of its redemption are gone." So the "fundamentalists" held strong in their belief in an infallible, divinely inspired Bible and defended the long-standing doctrines which had been drawn from it. Conversely, mainline denominations were moved by the new scholarship and have since reinterpreted, left behind, or just gone mute on many of the traditional (and fundamental) doctrines, such as the Fall, original sin, the virgin birth, atonement, salvation, and hell.

If you happen to attend a service at a mainline church, you are not likely to hear much about the need to be saved or Jesus' atoning death on the cross. The pastor will likely focus on Jesus' life as a model for treating others better or on Bible verses that can support stewardship of our planet. Christianity essentially serves as an entry point for promoting social and environmental justice.

Of course Evangelical Christians also celebrate Jesus' earthly deeds and teachings, but they sure don't appreciate Jesus being treated as just a "good role model" or a "great teacher." First and foremost, he is the Son of God (and also God himself), who died for your sins so you don't have to go to hell anymore.

Liberal theology has been thinned out to the point where the same message could be comfortably delivered in a non-Christian setting. One might find similar nourishment from a

Native American legend, Hindu scripture, or an inspiring documentary. Mainline churches are left with a very worldly message — one about this life, not the next.

This by no means negates the value some churchgoers derive from the Christian tradition. One might hold a vague belief in a higher power or appreciate some of Jesus' teachings, but have little interest in defined Christian doctrine. One might believe this is just one of many faith traditions that can facilitate personal reflection, a sense of appreciation, or even community involvement. For many churchgoers this is what they want from the church experience. Great! I would just note that having appreciation for parts of the Christian tradition is not the same as believing Christianity makes sense.

ABOUT THE AUTHOR

www.evandavids.com

Made in the USA
San Bernardino, CA
08 May 2018